CRYPTO
INVESTING
FOR BEGINNERS

*Master Bitcoin, Ethereum, and
Altcoins with Expert Strategies and
Insights to Maximize Your Profits*

Mark Swanson

Table of Contents

CRYPTOCURRENCY INVESTING FOR BEGINNERS

BITCOIN INVESTING FOR BEGINNERS

CRYPTOCURRENCY INVESTING FOR BEGINNERS

Unlock Digital Wealth with Bitcoin, Ethereum, Altcoins, and DeFi

Introduction

In just over a decade, cryptocurrency has exploded from a digital curiosity into a volatile but legitimate financial phenomenon Bitcoin, the first and most well-known cryptocurrency, was valued at fractions of a penny when it was introduced in 2009. Fast forward to today, and it has hit peaks of nearly $60,000 per unit. This meteoric rise is a clear indicator of not just the potential financial rewards of investing in digital currencies but also the broader shift towards a digital economy.

I've been engrossed in the world of cryptocurrency since its formative years. With a background in finance and a deep-seated passion for demystifying complex technologies, I've dedicated myself to helping you—whether you're a veteran investor or a curious novice—understand and navigate the ever-evolving landscape of digital currencies. My goal is not just to inform you but to empower you to make intelligent, secure investments in this dynamic market.

This book is designed to peel back the layers of what often appears to be a complex and intimidating subject—cryptocurrency investing. By breaking down complex concepts into understandable terms, I aim to provide you with the knowledge needed to participate with confidence in the digital economy. From understanding the basic technology of blockchain to learning how to safely buy and trade various cryptocurrencies, this guide covers all you need to know to start building your digital asset portfolio.

As we delve into the world of cryptocurrency together, we'll confront and debunk common myths that might have made you hesitant about digital currencies. Cryptocurrencies are not just tools for illicit trade; they are being integrated into global financial systems. By the end of this book, you'll see that digital currencies are just as much a part of our economic reality as stocks and bonds.

What sets this book apart is its focus on security and practical advice. Illustrated with real-world examples, it offers step-by-step guidance on how to make prudent investment decisions, drawing on the latest research and expert insights. This book is tailored for readers of all ages, making complex content accessible to everyone, from teens to adults.

Approach this journey with an open mind and a cautious attitude. The world of cryptocurrency is rapidly evolving, and while it offers significant opportunities, it is not without risks. Use the insights from this book to weigh your decisions and invest wisely.

Let's begin this exciting journey into the future of finance. With the proper knowledge and tools at your disposal, you are well on your way to potentially reaping the benefits of your investments in the digital age. Let this be your guide to navigating the vibrant and sometimes volatile world of cryptocurrency investing.

Chapter 1

Understanding the Basics of Cryptocurrency

Did you know that if you had invested just $100 in Bitcoin back in 2010, your investment would have soared to well over $48 million by the end of 2017? This staggering fact isn't just a testament to Bitcoin's exceptional rise; it also illustrates the immense potential of cryptocurrencies. As you step into the world of digital currencies, it's crucial to grasp the foundational concepts that underpin this innovative financial landscape. This chapter aims to demystify the basic principles of cryptocurrency, making it accessible and engaging for you, regardless of your background in finance or technology.

What is Cryptocurrency? A Simple Explanation

Definition and Origin

Cryptocurrency is defined as a virtual and/or digital currency that uses cryptography for security. Unlike traditional currencies issued by governments (fiat currencies), cryptocurrencies operate by utilizing a decentralized network of computers. This decentralization is possible thanks to a technology called blockchain, which we'll explore more in the following sections.

Cryptocurrency was first described in a 2008 paper by either an individual or group using the pseudonym Satoshi Nakamoto. The first cryptocurrency, Bitcoin, was created as a peer-to-peer electronic cash system—free from control by any institution or government. This revolutionary idea not only introduced the world to Bitcoin but also laid the foundational principles for the many other digital currencies that would follow.

Key Characteristics

Cryptocurrencies share several key characteristics:

- Decentralization: Unlike centralized banking systems, where a central authority controls and issues currency, cryptocurrencies are managed by a network system of computers known as nodes. This network works on a peer-to-peer basis, making digital currencies less vulnerable to single points of failure and censorship.

- Immutability: Once the blockchain has recorded a transaction, it cannot be altered. This immutability is ensured through cryptographic hash functions, which secure the integrity of transaction histories.

- Transparency: Each transaction on the blockchain can be seen by every participant and cannot be changed. This helps build trust among users and makes it extremely difficult to cheat the system.

Bitcoin, the first and most well-known cryptocurrency, embodies all of these principles and remains the gold standard for evaluating other digital currencies.

Use Cases

The use of cryptocurrencies has grown exponentially, extending far beyond mere investment vehicles. Here are a few practical examples:

- Online Buying: Numerous online retailers and service providers will accept cryptocurrencies such as Bitcoin, Ethereum, and others as payment, offering a secure and often cheaper alternative to credit cards or PayPal.

- Remittances: Cryptocurrencies can significantly reduce the cost and increase the speed of sending money across borders. This is particularly beneficial for migrants sending remittances back to their home countries, as it bypasses expensive and slow traditional banking services.

- Investment Vehicles: Many people buy cryptocurrencies as investments, hoping that their value will increase over time. Cryptocurrencies have also given rise to new forms of investment strategies, such as initial coin offerings (ICOs) and token sales, where investors can buy into a new cryptocurrency before it hits the market.

Advantages Over Fiat

There are several advantages to using cryptocurrencies instead of traditional fiat currencies:

- Lower Fees: Without the need for intermediaries like banks, cryptocurrency transactions can have significantly lower fees in comparison to traditional bank transfers or credit card payments.

- Accessibility: Cryptocurrencies can be particularly empowering for the population without traditional bank accounts by providing access to financial services.

- Privacy: While not wholly anonymous, cryptocurrency transactions offer greater privacy compared to traditional financial transactions, as they do not require personal information to be completed.

Blockchain Basics: How Transactions Work

Imagine a world where every financial transaction you make, from buying a coffee to selling a used textbook, is recorded in a massive ledger that is visible to everyone but owned by none. This isn't a scene from a futuristic movie; this is the reality of blockchain technology, the backbone of cryptocurrency systems. Blockchain acts as a distributed ledger, a database that is shared, replicated, and synchronized among the members of a decentralized network. The genius of blockchain is not just its ability to keep records; it's how it records and links information through cryptography, making it secure and unchangeable without the need for a central authority.

When you initiate a cryptocurrency transaction, you are essentially creating a digital 'statement,' saying, "I am sending this amount of cryptocurrency to this person." Here's where it gets interesting. Each user, or 'node.' on the cryptocurrency network has a wallet, which can be thought of as a personal ledger. Each wallet has one or more pairs of private and public keys. The public key is what you share with others to receive funds, while the private key is what you guard zealously, as it's used to approve transactions and prove ownership of the funds you are sending.

The transaction you initiate is then broadcast to the network, where it waits in a pool of unconfirmed transactions. This is where 'miners' come into play. Mining involves complex puzzles that nodes or 'miners' solve using high-powered computers. The first miner to solve the puzzle is able to add transactions to the blockchain. This process is part of what is known as the Proof of Work (PoW) consensus mechanism and is used to confirm transactions and introduce new blocks to the chain. Another mechanism, called Proof of Stake (PoS), selects validators in proportion to the number of holdings in the cryptocurrency. Both these mechanisms ensure that all transactions are verified and agreed upon by the network without the need for central oversight, thus maintaining the integrity and security of the blockchain.

Security in blockchain technology is paramount and is maintained through cryptographic hashing. Each block contains a cryptographical hash of the previous block, timestamp, and transaction data. This linkage between blocks means that to alter a single block, an attacker would need to change all subsequent blocks, which is practically impossible due to the immense amount of computational power required. This structure not only defends against fraudulent transactions but also makes the blockchain transparent and auditable by anyone in the network.

Blockchain's impact extends far beyond simply powering cryptocurrencies. Its attributes of decentralization, immutability, and transparency solve many issues of traditional transaction systems and have the potential for applications across various sectors, such as healthcare for maintaining patient records, supply chain management to track the authenticity of goods, or electoral systems to ensure secure and transparency in voting processes. This revolutionary technology fosters a level of trust and cooperation without the need for intermediaries, potentially redefining interactions in the global economy.

The Evolution of Cryptocurrencies: From Bitcoin to Today

The story of cryptocurrency begins not with a bang but with a quiet post on an obscure mailing list by someone under the name Satoshi Nakamoto. In 2008, this person or group of people issued a white paper: "Bitcoin: A Peer-to-Peer Electronic Cash System." This document laid out the mechanics of what would become the first cryptocurrency, Bitcoin. It proposed a system using a decentralized ledger—the blockchain—to record transactions securely and anonymously, bypassing traditional financial intermediaries. This was a revolutionary idea, aiming to democratize finance and reduce dependency on central banks and governments. Bitcoin officially came into existence in January 2009 with the mining of the Genesis Block.

As Bitcoin began to gain traction, it opened the floodgates for other digital currencies, collectively known as altcoins. Each of these sought to improve or diversify Bitcoin's original premise. For instance, Ethereum, introduced by Vitalik Buterin in 2015, added the capability for smart contracts, which automate transactions when certain conditions are met. Ethereum broadened the scope of blockchain applications, paving the way for decentralized finance (DeFi) and non-fungible tokens (NFTs). Ripple, another significant cryptocurrency, focused on solving problems related to international money transfers, offering a faster and more efficient alternative to systems like SWIFT. These developments marked not just technological advancements but also a growing recognition of the potential of cryptocurrencies to reshape various aspects of financial and commercial activities.

The impact of cryptocurrencies on financial markets has been profound and multifaceted. Initially viewed with skepticism, cryptocurrencies have gradually gained acceptance among both retail and institutional investors. They are now seen as a legitimate asset class, with major financial firms offering cryptocurrency-related products such as futures, options, and exchange-traded funds (ETFs). This mainstream acceptance has helped increase the liquidity and stability of cryptocurrency markets. However, it has also led to increased scrutiny from regulators and policymakers concerned about potential risks, including market volatility, investor protection, and misuse for illicit activities.

The regulatory scene for cryptocurrencies has evolved significantly over the years. Different countries have taken diverse approaches, ranging from outright bans to enthusiastic adoption. For instance, Japan recognized Bitcoin as a legal payment method in 2017, which boosted its use in the country. On the other hand, China has taken a stricter stance, cracking down on cryptocurrency trading and mining due to concerns about financial risk and energy consumption. In the United States, the regulatory environment has been somewhat ambiguous, with various federal agencies applying differing definitions and rules. The Securities and Exchange Commission (SEC), for example, has been scrutinizing ICOs and token sales to determine whether they should be classified and regulated as securities. The evolution of these regulations is a critical area of interest for investors and industry participants, as it significantly affects the development and adoption of cryptocurrency technologies.

Navigating these regulatory waters has become a key challenge for the crypto community. Each legal adjustment or new piece of legislation can send ripples across the market, influencing prices and shaping the development of new products and services. As cryptocurrencies continue to intersect more with traditional financial systems, the push and pull between innovation and regulation are likely to intensify. This dynamic creates a fascinating, albeit occasionally precarious, environment for investors and users, highlighting the need for ongoing education and cautious engagement with the crypto space.

Decoding Cryptocurrency Jargon: A Glossary for Beginners

Navigating the world of cryptocurrency can sometimes feel like learning a new language. From 'blockchain' to 'HODL,' each term carries a distinct meaning and implication that is crucial for understanding how digital currencies function and how you can interact with them effectively. Let's break down some of the key terms and phrases that are integral to mastering the language of cryptocurrencies.

Common Terms

- Blockchain: Think of it as a digital ledger or record book that is accessible to everyone but owned by no one. Every 'block' in the chain contains many transactions. Once a block is completed, it's added to the chain in a linear, chronological order. Blockchain's design makes it highly resistant to tampering, changing, or hacking.

- Mining: This is the process by which new cryptocurrency coins are made available, and transactions are verified and added to a blockchain. Miners use powerful computers to solve intricate mathematical problems that validate transactions. Successful miners are rewarded with new cryptocurrency tokens.

- Wallet: In cryptocurrency, a wallet is a digital means to store your coins securely. It's not like a physical wallet but rather a software program that holds your public and private keys, which allows you to receive and send cryptocurrencies and monitor your balance.

- Exchange: A platform allowing you to purchase, sell, or trade cryptocurrencies for additional digital currency or traditional currency, such as US dollars or Euros. These online marketplaces act like stock trading platforms.

- ICO (Initial Coin Offering): Similar to an Initial Public Offering (IPO) in the stock market. It's a way for cryptocurrency startups to raise money from the public by issuing a new token. Investors can buy these tokens, which might increase in value based on the success of the project.

Technical Concepts

- Hash Rate: This refers to the speed of a computer completing an operation in the cryptocurrency code. A higher hash rate increases the miners' opportunity to find the next block and receive a reward.

- Forks: In the cryptocurrency world, a fork happens when a blockchain's existing code is changed, resulting in two versions—one that follows the old rules and one that follows the new rules. This can be a result of disagreements within the community on certain changes in the protocol.

- Smart Contracts: These are self-executing contracts wherein an agreement's terms between the buyer and seller are written directly into the lines of code. The code and the agreements contained therein exist across a distributed, decentralized blockchain network. Smart contracts permit trusted deals to be conducted between disparate and unidentified parties without the need for a central authority, legal system, or external enforcement mechanism.

- Layer Solutions: These are technologies developed to improve the scalability and speed of blockchains. Layers built on top of existing blockchain systems provide higher transaction speeds and better scaling options.

Investment Terms

- HODL: Originally a typo for "hold" in an online forum, HODL has become a backronym for "Hold On for Dear Life." It represents a passive investment strategy where you hold onto your cryptocurrency investments despite price volatility.

- Bear/Bull Market: These terms are borrowed from the stock market. A bear market means that a market is declining, while a bull market refers to one that is rising. In the cryptocurrency context, bulls believe that the prices of specific currencies will increase, while bears believe the opposite.

- FOMO (Fear of Missing Out): The fear is that an exciting or thought-provoking event may be occurring elsewhere. This often originates in posts seen on social media. In crypto, it refers to the fear of not buying a token that might skyrocket in value.

- Whale: This term is used to describe individuals or entities that hold large amounts of cryptocurrency. These Whales have enough market power to influence the cryptocurrency market.

Security Terms

- Private Key: A sophisticated form of cryptography that permits a user to access their cryptocurrency. It's essentially your digital signature, and you should guard it with your life. If someone else obtains your private key, they can steal your crypto.

- Public Key: This acts like your bank account number. It's a way to identify your wallet so that you can receive coins. Unlike your private key, your public key is meant to be shared.

- Multi-signature Wallets: These require multiple keys to authorize a cryptocurrency transaction rather than a single signature from one key, offering added security.

- Cold Storage: This refers to keeping your cryptocurrency completely offline, which usually can be achieved through hardware wallets, USB drives, or even paper wallets. This method is particularly useful for protecting large amounts of cryptocurrency from hacking or other online threats.

Navigating through the maze of cryptocurrency terms is not just about adding new words to your vocabulary. Understanding these concepts opens up new vistas in the financial landscape, allowing you to make more informed decisions and better understand the discussions that shape the future of money. Whether you're planning to invest, use, or simply understand cryptocurrencies, getting familiar with this jargon is an invaluable part of your digital currency education.

How Cryptocurrencies Differ from Traditional Banking

The traditional banking system, as we know it, operates on a centralized model. This means that all financial transactions pass through a central authority—typically a bank or a financial institution. These entities control the flow of money, maintain transaction records, and are responsible for the security of these transactions. In contrast, cryptocurrencies introduce a decentralized model where control and verification are spread across a network of computers. This fundamental difference isn't just technical; it affects everything from how transactions are processed to how users interact with their money.

In a centralized banking system, the bank holds and controls your money. They have the authority to freeze accounts, dictate the terms of their services, and often charge fees for transactions. This centralized control also means that all your transactions are monitored by the bank and potentially by governmental bodies. Cryptocurrencies, on the other hand, offer a decentralized approach. When you use Bitcoin or any other cryptocurrency, you interact directly with the network, not a central authority. This setup empowers users with direct control over their transactions. You are able to send funds to anyone anywhere in the world without asking permission from a bank or paying exorbitant fees. This autonomy is particularly appealing in regions where the populace may not have access to traditional banking services or where the trust in financial institutions is low.

Let's talk about the efficiency of transactions. It can take days for traditional bank transfers to process, especially if they cross international borders, as they involve multiple parties and layers of bureaucracy. On top of that, each intermediary in the process adds their own transaction fees. Cryptocurrency transactions streamline this process. Because they are processed on the blockchain network, they can be completed more quickly—often within minutes—even if the transaction is international. As for the costs, because there are no middlemen setting fees, transaction fees for cryptocurrencies are typically much lower compared to traditional bank fees. This makes cryptocurrencies an attractive alternative for both everyday transactions and international remittances.

Global accessibility is another significant advantage of cryptocurrencies over traditional banking. According to the World Bank, globally, an estimated 1.7 billion adults have no access to a bank account. The reasons range from lack of sufficient funds and high fees to the geographical inaccessibility of banking services. Cryptocurrencies can change this dynamic because all you need to carry out transactions is an internet connection and a digital wallet. This accessibility has the potential to empower millions by bringing them into the global economy, fostering greater financial inclusion and independence.

Moreover, cryptocurrencies can serve regions and communities historically neglected or underserved by traditional financial systems. For instance, small business owners in remote or rural areas can accept payments in cryptocurrencies, bypassing the need for credit card processors or the high fees associated with them. Non-governmental organizations (NGOs) working in crisis-stricken regions use cryptocurrencies to transfer funds quickly and securely to areas where banking infrastructure is damaged or non-existent. This highlights not just the technical advantages of cryptocurrencies but their potential to create more equitable financial opportunities.

Cryptocurrencies are reshaping financial transactions with their decentralized nature, empowering users with more control and offering unparalleled accessibility. As we continue to explore the capabilities and potential of digital currencies, it's clear that they offer a compelling alternative to traditional banking, particularly in facilitating faster, cheaper, and more inclusive financial services. This evolution in how we think about and manage money reflects a broader shift towards a more interconnected and equitable global financial system.

Chapter 2

Setting Up for Investment Success

Imagine stepping into the world of cryptocurrency, where possibilities abound, and the promise of financial evolution is just a few clicks away. But before you dive into buying your first digital coin, you need a safe place to store it. Enter the realm of cryptocurrency wallets. Much like your physical wallet holds your cash and cards, a cryptocurrency wallet is essential for managing your digital assets. But unlike the leather-bound wallet in your pocket, digital wallets come in several forms, each with its unique features and security measures. In this chapter, we'll guide you through choosing your first cryptocurrency wallet, ensuring you start your crypto journey on the right foot.

Choosing Your First Cryptocurrency Wallet

Types of Wallets

Cryptocurrency wallets can broadly be categorized into three types: hardware, software, and paper wallets. Each type serves the same purpose but in a slightly different way, and understanding these differences is critical to choosing the right one for you.

- Hardware Wallets: Think of these as your personal crypto vaults. Small, portable devices that look much like USB drives, hardware wallets store your private keys offline, making them immune to online hacking attempts. They are considered the most secure type of wallet, especially for holding large amounts of cryptocurrency over an extended period. However, they can be a bit expensive, and their physical nature means they can be lost or damaged.

- Software Wallets: These are apps or programs that can be downloaded to your personal computer or phone. They are convenient for actively trading or spending your cryptocurrencies, as they are easily accessible. However, they are less secure than hardware wallets because they remain connected to the Internet, exposing them to potential cyber threats. Software wallets are generally free, which makes them a good option for beginners looking to start small.

- Paper Wallets: The simplest form of a cryptocurrency wallet, a paper wallet is literally just a piece of paper on which your cryptocurrency addresses and private keys are printed. They are completely offline, which makes them highly secure from online hacking. However, paper wallets are susceptible to risks like being lost, damaged, or even stolen. They are not as convenient for quick or frequent transactions and require a high level of responsibility in safeguarding them.

Security Features

When it comes to cryptocurrencies, security cannot be overstated. Here are some critical security features to look for in a wallet:

- Two-Factor Authentication (2FA): This adds an additional layer of security by necessitating not only a password and username but also something that only the user has on them, i.e., a piece of information only they should know or have immediately to hand—often a physical token.

- Multi-Signature Options: Often referred to as multisig, this feature requires multiple keys to authorize a single cryptocurrency transaction. It's like having a bank safe that needs two or three keys to open. This is particularly useful for business accounts or joint accounts, providing an extra layer of security by ensuring one person does not have complete control over the wallet's funds.

- Backup and Recovery Procedures: Always choose a wallet that offers robust backup and recovery options. Being able to recover your wallet is crucial if you forget your password or, worse, lose your device. Most wallets provide a recovery phrase—a series of words generated at random—which you must write down and store securely. This phrase is used to restore your wallet and recover your funds if needed.

Choosing the Right Wallet

Selecting the right wallet depends largely on how you plan to use your cryptocurrency. Consider the following criteria:

- Security: As discussed, the level of security is paramount. Hardware wallets offer the best security for large amounts of cryptocurrencies or long-term investments.

- User-Friendliness: Especially important for beginners, the wallet's interface should be easy to understand and navigate.

- Support for Multiple Currencies: If you plan to deal in various cryptocurrencies, look for a wallet that supports multiple currencies. This saves you the hassle of managing different wallets for different coins.

- Customer Support: Great customer support is invaluable when you're new to crypto. Check if the wallet provider offers prompt and reliable support.

Setting Up a Wallet

Setting up a cryptocurrency wallet is your first active step into the world of digital currencies. Here's how you can get started:

1. Choose Your Wallet: Based on your needs and the factors we discussed, select the type of wallet you want to use.

2. Download/Install the Wallet: For software wallets, download the app or program from a trusted source and install it on your device. Make sure you purchase your hardware wallet from a reputable vendor.

3. Set Up Security Measures: Configure all security settings available, especially 2FA and backup options. Make sure your recovery phrase is stored in a safe place.

4. Transfer Funds: Once your wallet is secure, you can transfer your cryptocurrency into it from an exchange or another wallet.

5. Keep Your Software Updated: If you're using a software wallet, regularly check and install updates to ensure your wallet's software is up to date with the latest security enhancements.

Choosing the right wallet is like finding the perfect home for your digital currencies. It's not just about keeping them safe; it's about making your experience in the crypto world as smooth and hassle-free as possible. With the right wallet in hand, you're now ready to start exploring the vast opportunities of cryptocurrency investing.

Essential Security Measures for Crypto Investors

When you step into the vibrant world of cryptocurrency, think of security as your best friend—the one who keeps you safe and guards your secrets. In this case, your 'secrets' are your investments and access keys, and your 'friend' is the robust security measure you set up to protect them. Cryptocurrency, by its very nature, offers a level of security inherently through blockchain technology. Still, fundamental safeguarding begins with how you manage your assets and interactions in the digital space.

Understanding Crypto Security

The first rule of crypto security is understanding that you are primarily responsible for it. Unlike traditional banking systems, where you can often rely on institutions to step in if things go wrong, the decentralized nature of cryptocurrencies means the onus is on you to maintain security. This begins with a clear grasp of what security in the crypto world entails—keeping your private keys private, being vigilant against scams, and regularly updating and auditing your security practices. Private keys are akin to the most personal piece of information you can hold because they provide access to your cryptocurrencies. Think of them as the combination to a safe where your digital assets are stored. Losing them to negligence or theft isn't just about losing digital data; it's about losing real money.

Protecting Private Keys

Protecting your private keys is the cornerstone of your crypto security plan. Here are some strategies to ensure they remain safe from unauthorized access:

- Use Encrypted Storage: Always store your keys in encrypted storage. This means even if someone were to gain access to your storage, deciphering your keys without the encryption key would be incredibly challenging.

- Avoid Sharing: Keep your keys confidential. The fewer people who know about where and how you store your private keys, the better.

- Physical Security: For keys stored on physical devices or paper, ensure they are kept in a secure location, such as a safe or a safety deposit box. Environmental factors like water or fire can also pose risks, so consider protective cases for added security.

- Regular Updates: Just as you might change the locks on your home if keys are lost or stolen, regularly updating your digital 'locks' or access methods can help protect against theft.

Avoiding Phishing and Scams

Phishing attacks and scams are unfortunately common in the cryptocurrency world, often designed to trick you into giving away your private keys or sending funds to fraudulent operators. Staying safe means staying informed:

- Know Common Scams: Familiarize yourself with the types of scams that are prevalent in the crypto space. These can range from fake ICOs promising incredible returns to phishing emails pretending to be from legitimate sources asking for your keys.

- Verify Sources: Always double-check the URLs of websites and the identity of people you interact with online. Scammers often create fake websites and profiles that look remarkably real.

- Think Before You Click: Be wary of links in emails or messages, especially if they ask for urgent action like providing passwords or sending funds. If you have doubts, visit the official website directly by typing the URL manually.

Regular Security Audits

Just like any good security system, your crypto defenses need regular testing and updating to ensure they can stand up against new threats. Conducting regular security audits involves:

- Reviewing Your Security Practices: Periodically review how you store and manage your keys and consider if the measures you have in place still offer adequate protection. As technology evolves, so do the tools available to enhance security.

- Updating Software: Keep all software up-to-date, including wallet software and any applications associated with cryptocurrency management. Updates may include patches for security vulnerabilities that can be exploited by hackers.

- Testing Backup Systems: Regularly test any backup systems you have in place to ensure they work effectively and that you can recover your digital assets in case of a loss or failure.

These proactive steps don't just protect your investments; they also give you peace of mind, allowing you to engage with the crypto world with confidence, knowing you've done your best to secure your digital treasure. Don't forget that in the land of cryptocurrency, your security is only as strong as the weakest link in your defense strategy. Keeping that link fortified means staying vigilant, educated, and proactive about security at all times.

Understanding Crypto Exchanges: Where and How to Buy

Navigating the landscape of cryptocurrency exchanges can feel like exploring a bustling market where each stall has its unique set of offerings and rules. Essentially, these exchanges are platforms where you can buy, sell, or trade cryptocurrencies. However, not all exchanges are created equal; they come in various forms, each catering to different needs and preferences. Let's break down the three primary types of exchanges you'll encounter and what makes each of them tick.

Centralized Exchanges (CEXs) are the most prevalent and user-friendly type of crypto exchange. They are operated by companies that provide a platform for trading cryptocurrencies in exchange for fees. These are similar to traditional stock exchanges. They act as intermediaries in your trades, providing services like order matching, currency storage, and facilitating transactions. Users appreciate centralized exchanges for their high liquidity, meaning you can buy and sell large amounts of cryptocurrency relatively easily. They also offer more advanced trading options like futures and margin trading. However, their central control becomes a double-edged sword; it introduces risks like hacking, as seen in numerous security breaches over the years. Furthermore, since they hold your funds, there's a level of trust you need to place in their security measures and business stability.

Decentralized Exchanges (DEXs) offer a stark contrast by allowing direct peer-to-peer transactions online without needing an intermediary. Here, the trades occur directly between users (peer-to-peer) through an automated process. This setup enhances security because your funds are not held by the exchange, they stay in your wallet until the transaction is executed. It also means better privacy since personal data isn't required to sign up. However, decentralized exchanges can be less user-friendly and often suffer from low liquidity and slower trade execution, which might not be ideal for those looking to make quick trades or large orders.

Hybrid Exchanges attempt to blend the best features of both centralized and decentralized exchanges. They aim to provide the liquidity and speed of a CEX with the security and anonymity of a DEX. These platforms are relatively new and are still evolving, but they represent a promising direction for secure and efficient crypto trading.

When choosing an exchange, consider several factors to ensure it meets your needs. Security is paramount; look for exchanges that employ strong security measures. For example, encryption, cold storage of funds, and two-factor authentication. Liquidity is crucial, too; a more liquid market makes it easier to trade cryptocurrencies without affecting their price too much. Fees vary significantly between exchanges and can substantially impact the cost of trading, especially if you plan to trade often or in large volumes. Lastly, user experience can dramatically influence your trading success; a well-designed interface and good customer support can enhance your trading experience.

Now, let's walk through the typical process of buying cryptocurrency on an exchange:

1. Set Up an Account: First, you need to create an account on the exchange: provide your email address, create a password, and sometimes verify your identity (known as KYC – Know Your Customer procedures), which may require a photo ID and proof of residency.

2. Fund Your Account: After your account is set up and verified, you'll need to deposit funds. Most exchanges will accept bank transfers and credit card payments, and some even support PayPal. Choose the method that aligns with your convenience and cost considerations.

3. Make a Purchase: With your account funded, you can now buy cryptocurrency. This typically involves selecting the type of currency you want to buy, specifying the amount, and executing the transaction. Some exchanges offer a simple 'buy/sell' interface, while others provide advanced trading tools and charts for more strategic trading.

4. Withdraw and Transfer: After purchasing, it's advisable to withdraw your cryptocurrency to a private wallet. Leaving your crypto in an exchange's wallet puts you at risk of losing your cryptocurrency should the exchange be hacked or go out of business. To withdraw, you'll just need to enter your private wallet's address and transfer the funds.

Navigating crypto exchanges doesn't have to be intimidating. By understanding the types of exchanges and what to look for when choosing one, you're better equipped to engage with the crypto market safely and effectively. Remember, the right exchange for you depends on your specific needs, trading style, and security preferences. Whether you opt for the convenience of a centralized exchange, the security of a decentralized exchange, or the balanced approach of a hybrid, you're now ready to take the next step in your cryptocurrency investment adventure.

Verifying Sources: Spotting Reliable Crypto Information

In the dynamic world of cryptocurrency, where fortunes can seemingly be made overnight, the information you rely on can be your greatest asset or your most significant liability. With the rapid proliferation of digital currencies and blockchain technology, there's a parallel rise in the volume of information available—some of it helpful, much of it noise, and some potentially misleading or even harmful. As an investor, whether novice or seasoned, your ability to critically assess the reliability and bias of information sources is crucial. It's akin to developing a finely tuned filter that separates the signal from the noise, ensuring you base your decisions on information that is not only accurate but also unbiased and relevant.

When evaluating sources of cryptocurrency information, consider their history, reputation, and transparency. Reliable sources typically have a track record of factual accuracy and are upfront about their ownership, funding, and editorial process. They often cite reputable sources themselves and are written by authors whose credentials and affiliations are clear and relevant to the field of cryptocurrency. Watch out for red flags such as a lack of transparency about the author or the organization, overly sensational headlines, and articles that rely heavily on anonymous sources or that fail to cite sources altogether.

Another critical skill is distinguishing between fact-based reporting and speculative hype. The crypto world is particularly rife with speculation, partly due to its relative novelty and the high volatility of digital currencies. While speculation about future prices or the potential impact of new technologies is a staple of financial reporting, it should not be confused with factual information about current events. Articles and reports should make a clear distinction between what is known and confirmed and what is conjecture or opinion. Be wary of content that presents speculative predictions with the same certainty as established facts or that bases sweeping statements on unverifiable or anonymous sources.

In terms of practical tools for verifying the credibility of cryptocurrency news, analysis, and advice, several online resources can be beneficial. Websites like CoinMarketCap provide comprehensive data on market capitalizations, pricing, and volume for various cryptocurrencies, which can help verify claims made in articles. Blockchain explorers such as Etherscan or Blockchain.com allow you to track specific transactions and view the history and distribution of blockchain assets, providing a factual basis to verify claims about transaction volumes or the movement of funds. Additionally, forums like Reddit or specialized platforms like CryptoCompare can offer community-driven insights and feedback on various sources and pieces of news.

Building a trusted resource list is an ongoing process that can significantly enhance your understanding and engagement with the cryptocurrency market. Start by identifying a few key websites, podcasts, and others with a proven track record for reliability and depth. Regularly engage with their content and monitor the accuracy of their predictions and analysis. Over time, expand your list based on references from these trusted sources or by using aggregation platforms like Feedly to discover and track new and relevant voices in the space. Remember, the goal is not to build an echo chamber but to cultivate a diverse portfolio of reliable sources that can provide you with a well-rounded view of the crypto world. This approach not only helps you stay informed but also protects you from the pitfalls of misinformation that can lead to costly investment mistakes.

Investment Mindset: Preparing for Volatility in Crypto Markets

When stepping into the ever-turbulent waters of cryptocurrency investing, understanding and preparing for market volatility is akin to wearing a life vest. The price fluctuations in crypto markets can be dizzying, with significant swings occurring within hours or even minutes. Several factors contribute to this high volatility. Firstly, the cryptocurrency market is relatively young, and with less historical data available, predictions and reactions can be extreme. Additionally, the market is heavily influenced by news and events, which can lead to rapid speculative trading. The decentralized nature of cryptocurrencies also means that regulatory news from different countries can impact prices in unpredictable ways.

For many, the rollercoaster-like nature of crypto markets can be emotionally overwhelming. It's easy to get caught up in the excitement of a surge or the panic of a drop. Here lies the importance of emotional resilience—maintaining a steady hand regardless of market conditions. Developing this strength requires a clear understanding of your investment goals and a commitment to not make impulsive decisions based on fleeting market trends. Emotional resilience in investing is about sticking to a well-considered strategy, even when your instincts might urge you to run with the crowd.

Risk management is another critical aspect of navigating crypto investments wisely. Diversification is a fundamental strategy here; don't put all your eggs in one basket. If you spread your investments across diverse assets, you can mitigate the risk of a substantial loss if one investment fails. Setting stop losses is another strategy that can help protect your investments. This involves setting a predetermined level at which your asset will be sold to prevent further loss, helping you manage and contain potential losses effectively. Moreover, it's crucial to only invest what you can afford to lose. The high volatility of the market means that investments can lead to substantial gains but also significant losses, sometimes very quickly.

Adopting a long-term perspective can also serve as a stabilizing force. While the crypto market is known for its rapid gains, it's essential to focus on steady growth over time. This perspective helps in smoothing out the highs and lows and reduces the temptation to react hastily to short-term movements. Long-term investing means being patient and waiting for your investments to mature over time, which historically has been a more successful approach than trying to time the market for quick gains.

Navigational tools and strategies such as these not only prepare you to better handle the volatility of the crypto market but also equip you to make more informed, rational investment decisions. Adopting a disciplined approach to investing, grounded in a solid understanding of market dynamics and personal risk tolerance, sets a foundation that can withstand the pressures of market fluctuations and the noise of passing trends.

In conclusion, entering the crypto market with a prepared mindset can make the difference between a precarious gamble and a calculated investment strategy.

Understanding the inherent volatility, practicing emotional resilience, applying risk management techniques, and maintaining a long-term perspective are crucial steps in cultivating a robust investment approach. As you continue to navigate through the complexities of cryptocurrency investing, these strategies will not only safeguard your investments but also onhance your overall experience in the digital finance landscape.

Moving forward, the next chapter will delve deeper into the specific tools and strategies that will help you optimize your investment decisions and manage your portfolio more effectively. By building on the foundational knowledge and mindset strategies discussed here, you'll be better equipped to engage with the dynamic world of cryptocurrencies, making investment choices that will align with your long-term financial goals.

Chapter 3

Investing Strategies for Beginners

Imagine you're in a bustling market—the colors, the noise, the myriad of options. This is somewhat like entering the cryptocurrency market, but instead of fruits and fabrics, you're dealing with a vibrant array of digital currencies, each with its potential highs and lows. Now, how do you make sense of all this? How do you pick the ripe fruits and avoid the rotten ones? This chapter is your guide to understanding and navigating the complex yet fascinating world of cryptocurrency markets. Here, we'll arm you with the basic tools and knowledge to start analyzing and making informed decisions in your investment journey.

Analyzing the Market: Basic Techniques for Beginners

Understanding the cryptocurrency market can seem daunting at first, but with the precise tools and a bit of practice, it becomes an engaging and insightful experience. Let's start with the basics—market indicators, which are essentially the vital signs of the market. These indicators include volume, price trends, and market capitalization.

Volume refers to the total number of coins that have been traded in a given timeframe. It is a powerful indicator of the activity level associated with a cryptocurrency. High trading volumes often indicate a high interest in the currency at its current price and can signify stability or potential upcoming changes in price due to increased buying or selling pressure.

Price trends provide insights into the momentum of a cryptocurrency's price. Is the price steadily increasing, or is it experiencing a downward spiral? Understanding these trends helps in predicting future movements and making decisions about when might be a good time to buy or sell.

Market capitalization, or market cap, is calculated by multiplying the current price of the currency by the total number of coins in circulation. It gives you an idea of the total value of all coins and helps gauge the scale and growth potential of the cryptocurrencies. Larger market caps usually indicate a safer investment as these markets are less susceptible to manipulation.

Now, let's talk about candlestick charts, a trader's best friend. These charts are named for their candle-like shapes, each candle providing four key pieces of information: the opening price, the closing price, the highest price, and the lowest price within a selected period. Candlestick patterns can give you insights into market sentiment and potential price movements. For example, a 'bullish engulfing' pattern suggests a potential rise, while a 'bearish engulfing' pattern might indicate a coming drop in price.

But it's not just about cold numbers and patterns; the cryptocurrency market is greatly influenced by news and global events. Regulatory changes, technological advancements, and significant shifts in investor sentiment can all dramatically affect the market. For instance, when a country announces a new regulatory framework for cryptocurrencies, it can lead to price volatility. Similarly, technological breakthroughs in blockchain, the technology underpinning cryptocurrencies, could lead to increased investor interest and a surge in price.

Sentiment Analysis

Finally, understanding market sentiment is crucial. This is the overall attitude of investors toward a particular cryptocurrency and is often influenced by news or the general economic environment. Tools, such as social media monitoring and sentiment analysis software, can help you gauge public opinion. For example, a sudden spike in positive tweets about a cryptocurrency can precede a rise in its price.

Long-term vs. Short-term Investments: Pros and Cons

Investing in cryptocurrencies can be akin to choosing between sprinting and running a marathon. Each approach, whether it's the rapid-fire trades of short-term investing or the patient journey of long-term investment, carries its own set of strategies, benefits, and challenges. Understanding these differences and determining which one aligns with your personal financial goals and lifestyle can significantly influence your success in the crypto markets.

Defining Investment Horizons

Firstly, it's crucial to understand what sets short-term and long-term investment strategies apart. Short-term investments typically refer to assets bought and sold within a short period, usually less than a year. Traders in this arena are often looking for quick profits from price fluctuations in the market. On the other hand, long-term investments are held for several years or even decades. Investors in this category are usually less concerned with short-term market volatility and more focused on the potential for substantial growth over time.

Benefits of Long-term Investing

Long-term investing in cryptocurrency can be particularly advantageous. One of the most significant benefits is the potential for higher returns. Cryptocurrencies, despite their volatility, have shown a general trend of substantial growth over the years. For instance, early investors in Bitcoin have seen their investments grow exponentially as the cryptocurrency has gained popularity and acceptance around the world. Moreover, long-term investments tend to mitigate the risks associated with the short-term volatility of the crypto market. By holding onto investments for a longer period, you're less affected by short-term fluctuations and can potentially ride out low periods until the market recovers.

Another advantage of long-term investing is the reduced impact of taxes. In many jurisdictions, long-term investments benefit from lower capital gains taxes compared to short-term investments. This can make a significant difference in your net returns. Additionally, long-term investing requires less time and energy on a day-to-day basis compared to short-term trading, which demands constant monitoring of the market and quick decision-making skills.

Risks and Rewards of Short-term Trading

While short-term trading can offer exciting opportunities for a quick profit, it also comes with its own set of challenges. The crypto market is especially unpredictable, and prices can swing wildly in short periods, making trading a high-stress endeavor. Successful short-term traders need to be skilled at reading market signals and must have the time to actively monitor trends. They also need to be disciplined enough to avoid emotional trading, which can lead to significant losses.

Moreover, short-term trading incurs higher transaction costs due to frequent buying and selling of assets. These costs can eat into your profits if not carefully managed. There's also the risk of significant losses if the market moves against you, especially if you're using leverage to increase your trading power. This can make short-term trading unsuitable for those who are risk-averse or new to cryptocurrencies.

Choosing Your Strategy

Deciding whether or not you're ready to pursue a long-term or short-term investment strategy in cryptocurrencies largely depends on your individual financial goals, risk tolerance, and time commitment. If you're looking to build wealth over time and can afford to wait out the market's ups and downs, long-term investing might be more suitable for you. This approach is generally less stressful and less time-consuming, allowing you to focus on other aspects of your life while your investments potentially grow.

Conversely, if you enjoy the thrill of trading and have the time to dedicate to studying the market and actively managing your investments, short-term trading could be rewarding. However, it's essential to have a clear strategy and to set rules for entering and exiting trades to manage risks effectively.

In either case, educating yourself about the market, staying updated with global events that could affect cryptocurrency prices, and using the right tools to analyze and manage your investments are crucial steps in achieving success. Whether you choose the sprint or the marathon, the key to profitability lies in understanding the nuances of your chosen investment horizon and aligning it with your financial vision.

Diversifying Your Crypto Portfolio to Mitigate Risks

When you first dip your toes into the vast ocean of cryptocurrency, the temptation to dive deep into popular coins like Bitcoin and Ethereum is quite strong. However, just as a diet rich in a variety of nutrients supports health, a well-diversified investment portfolio can be your best defense against the unpredictability of the market. Diversification in the context of crypto investing involves spreading your investment across different types of assets. This strategy not only minimizes your risk if one asset performs poorly but also positions you to potentially capture gains from multiple sources.

Diversification is rooted in the age-old adage, "Don't put all your eggs in one basket." In the volatile world of cryptocurrencies, this couldn't be more applicable. By diversifying, you reduce the impact that any single failing component can have on your overall portfolio. For instance, if you have invested only in Bitcoin and it experiences a sharp decline, your portfolio's value will plummet. However, if you have diversified across different asset types, a drop in Bitcoin's value might be offset by stability or gains in other crypto assets.

Let's explore the different categories of crypto assets that can add diversity to your portfolio:

- Stablecoins: These are cryptocurrencies that are pegged to a stable asset, including the US dollar, in order to maintain a consistent value. Examples include USDT (Tether), USDC (USD

Coin), and DAI. Including stablecoins in your portfolio can provide a buffer against the volatility typically associated with cryptocurrencies. They are particularly useful for managing the risks of trading and providing a safe haven during market downturns.

- Utility Tokens: Unlike coins like Bitcoin, which are primarily used as digital money, utility tokens allow users to access a product or service. These tokens are often used on decentralized applications (dApps). For example, Filecoin offers decentralized storage solutions, and its tokens are used to pay for services. Investing in utility tokens allows you to benefit from the growth of specific sectors within the blockchain ecosystem.

- Privacy Coins: These cryptocurrencies focus on providing users with greater anonymity and privacy when making transactions. Monero and Zcash are prominent examples of privacy coins. They use advanced cryptographic techniques to shield transaction details, making them attractive for users who prioritize privacy. Including privacy coins in your portfolio could hedge against potential regulations affecting more transparent cryptocurrencies.

Balancing your crypto portfolio involves more than just choosing different assets; it's about aligning your investment with your risk tolerance and goals. Start by assessing how much risk you're willing to take and what you aim to achieve with your investments. If you prefer lower risk, you might lean more towards stablecoins and established cryptocurrencies with a longer track record. Conversely, if you are inclined towards higher risk for potentially higher returns, emerging utility tokens or privacy coins might be more appealing.

Once you have selected a diverse set of assets, the next step is to decide how much to invest in each. A common strategy is to allocate larger portions to less volatile assets and smaller portions to higher-risk assets. This allocation should reflect your risk assessment and investment goals. Remember, the key is not just diversity but balance. Having a wide range of assets is futile if they don't collectively work towards achieving your financial objectives.

Rebalancing your portfolio regularly is crucial to maintaining this balance. Cryptocurrency markets can shift rapidly, and an asset that once constituted a small portion of your portfolio could grow to dominate it, skewing your intended asset allocation. When you rebalance, you ensure that your portfolio does not stray too far from your risk tolerance level. The frequency of rebalancing depends on the market's volatility and your personal investment strategy. Some investors rebalance quarterly, others bi-annually or annually. Monitoring market conditions and adjusting the frequency of your rebalancing can optimize your portfolio's performance and keep your investment strategy on track.

In essence, diversifying your crypto portfolio mitigates risk and maximizes the potential for returns. By understanding the different categories of crypto assets and strategically balancing and rebalancing your investments, you set a strong foundation for your financial growth in the crypto space. This approach not only shields you against the turbulence of a single cryptocurrency but also positions you to capitalize on opportunities across the broader crypto market.

When to Buy and When to Sell: Basic Timing Strategies

Navigating the highs and lows of the cryptocurrency market is a bit like surfing. You need to know when to paddle out and catch a wave and when it's time to ride it to shore. The trick isn't just about finding the biggest wave—it's about finding the right wave that matches your style and capabilities. In the world of crypto investments, this translates to understanding market timing, a skill that, when honed, can significantly enhance the effectiveness of your trading strategies.

Market timing is essentially the strategy of making buy or sell decisions of crypto assets by attempting to predict future market price movements. The goal is to buy at low prices and sell at high prices, but achieving this consistently over time is challenging, even for the most experienced traders. The volatility of cryptocurrency markets makes them particularly unpredictable. Therefore, it's crucial to emphasize strategy over luck, so instead of trying to perfectly time the market, which can be akin to catching lightning in a bottle, focus on developing a robust trading approach that will withstand the ups and downs, allowing you to make gains over the long term.

Implementing technical analysis tools can be immensely helpful in this regard. These tools analyze historical market data and attempt to forecast future market behavior based on patterns and indicators. For instance, moving averages is a popular tool that smooths out price data and creates a single flowing line, making it easier to identify a trend's direction. Similarly, the Relative Strength Index (RSI) can help determine whether a cryptocurrency is being overbought or oversold, suggesting potential reversal points. These tools don't provide a crystal ball into the future, but when used intelligently, they can offer valuable insights into potential market movements.

Another powerful technique in the arsenal of a crypto investor is dollar-cost averaging (DCA). This investment strategy involves regularly buying a fixed dollar amount of a particular investment, regardless of the share price, thereby reducing the impact of volatility on the overall purchase. The purchases occur at regular intervals and in equal amounts. If the market is down, your fixed dollar amount will buy more shares, and vice versa when the market is up. DCA can help lower the average cost per share of the investment over time, potentially reducing the risks and smoothing out the investment's performance. This is a particularly useful approach in the cryptocurrency market, known for its sharp highs and lows, as it mitigates the risk and takes the emotion out of investing.

Setting up buy or sell triggers can also streamline your trading decisions. These are automated rules that you set up on your trading platform to execute buy or sell orders when certain conditions are met. For example, you might set a buy trigger when a particular cryptocurrency drops to a specific price or a sell trigger when it rises to a certain price level. These triggers are based on your analysis and understanding of the market, and once set, they can help automate your trading strategy, allowing you to capitalize on market movements even when you're not actively monitoring the charts. This method not only saves time but also ensures that your emotions don't cloud your trading decisions.

Incorporating these strategies into your trading approach can help you make more informed and timely decisions and will enhance your ability to capitalize on market opportunities. While perfect timing is unattainable, equipping yourself with the right tools and strategies can increase your chances of success, making your trading journey not only more strategic but also more rewarding. Remember, in the fluctuating seas of cryptocurrency trading, using the correct navigational tools can make all the difference.

Using Tech Tools: Apps and Platforms for Market Analysis

In the vibrant and ever-evolving world of cryptocurrency, staying current with the newest market trends is critical. Thanks to technological advancements, a plethora of tools have been developed to aid investors in navigating these waters. These tools range from comprehensive desktop platforms to handy mobile apps, each equipped with a suite of features designed to streamline the analysis process. Understanding what each tool offers and how to effectively use them can significantly enhance your trading strategies and market understanding.

When exploring the landscape of market analysis tools, you'll encounter a variety of applications designed to cater to different aspects of trading and investment analysis. Popular platforms like TradingView and Coinigy are favorites among many traders for their in-depth charting capabilities and real-time data analytics. These platforms offer a broad range of features, including price charts for various cryptocurrencies, drawing tools, and even community forums where traders can exchange insights. Another helpful tool is CryptoCompare, which provides a comprehensive overview of cryptocurrency markets with data on price movements, volumes, and market cap across multiple exchanges.

Key features to look for in these tools include user-friendly interfaces that make navigation and comprehension easy, even for beginners. Alert systems are another essential feature; they notify you about significant price changes or when specific market conditions are met, helping you to act swiftly on potential trading opportunities. Integration with trading platforms is also a critical feature, allowing you to make trades directly from the analysis app. This integration streamlines the process, minimizing the time lag between decision-making and action, a crucial aspect in a market as volatile as cryptocurrency.

The choice between mobile and desktop applications depends mainly on your lifestyle and trading style. Mobile apps offer the advantage of accessibility and convenience. With a mobile app, you can monitor markets, execute trades, and receive alerts on the go, ensuring you never miss a beat, no matter where you are. Apps like Blockfolio and Delta are particularly popular among mobile users for their sleek interfaces and comprehensive tracking features that allow you to manage your portfolio from your smartphone.

However, desktop platforms often provide more robust analytics tools and a more stable environment for detailed analysis. They are particularly beneficial for those who engage in complex trading strategies that require multiple screens or detailed chart analyses. Desktop applications typically offer more charting options and a broader array of analytical tools compared to mobile apps, making them suitable for in-depth technical analysis.

Safety and security should never be compromised when choosing a tech tool for market analysis. The cryptocurrency market's decentralized nature makes it a prime target for cyber threats. Opt for platforms that prioritize security, offering features like two-factor authentication (2FA), encryption, and secure data storage. It's also prudent to conduct due diligence on the tool's developer, ensuring they have a solid reputation and a transparent privacy policy. Regularly updating the software is crucial to protect against vulnerabilities and ensure you are using the most secure and efficient version of the tool.

Incorporating these technological tools into your market analysis strategy can transform the way you interact with the cryptocurrency market. They not only provide you with real-time data and in-depth analysis but also enhance your decision-making process, allowing you to respond more effectively to market changes. As you become more familiar with these tools, you'll find yourself better equipped to manage your investments and capitalize on opportunities that you might have otherwise missed.

Navigating through the dynamic world of cryptocurrency can be daunting, but with the right tools at your disposal, it becomes a manageable and even enjoyable endeavor.

The tools and platforms discussed in this chapter are designed to enhance your understanding of the market, streamline your trading processes, and secure your transactions. From mobile apps that offer convenience and quick access to desktop platforms that provide comprehensive analysis and robust features, these technological solutions are invaluable for anyone looking to succeed in the crypto market.

As we wrap up this chapter, remember that the goal is to use these tools to inform and enhance your investment strategies, not to replace your judgment. Each tool offers different capabilities and may suit different trading styles and needs. Experiment with a variety of tools to find what works best for you, and always stay informed about new technological advancements that could further optimize your trading experience.

Looking ahead, the next chapter will delve into the psychological aspects of trading, exploring how emotions can influence decision-making and how to cultivate a mindset that fosters successful investment strategies. This exploration is crucial, as the mental and emotional demands of trading can be just as challenging as the technical aspects covered so far.

Chapter 4

Dealing with Risks and Scams

Navigating the exhilarating world of cryptocurrency is a lot like exploring uncharted waters—thrilling and potentially rewarding, but not without inherent risks. As you chart your course through these digital seas, it's crucial to be aware of the pirates lurking in the shadows: scams and fraudulent schemes that aim to part you from your hard-earned treasure. In this chapter, we'll delve deep into the common pitfalls that every cryptocurrency investor should be wary of and equip you with the tools and knowledge to steer clear of them. By understanding these risks, you'll be better prepared to safeguard your investments and navigate your way to safer harbors.

Identifying and Avoiding Common Cryptocurrency Scams

Types of Scams

The world of cryptocurrency, while full of opportunities, is also a fertile ground for various types of scams. These fraudulent activities can vary widely in their approach and sophistication, but some of the most common include:

- Phishing Scams: These occur when scammers create fake websites or send emails that mimic legitimate businesses to steal personal information or login credentials. They often urge you to act quickly, offering a false sense of urgency to trick you into providing sensitive information.

- Fake ICOs: Initial Coin Offerings (ICOs) can be an authentic way for new projects to raise funds. However, counterfeit ICOs are set up by scammers who use the hype around new launches to lure investors into buying nonexistent tokens. These can often be spotted by their lack of detailed documentation or unrealistic promises about returns.

- Ponzi Schemes: In a Ponzi scheme, returns are paid to earlier investors using the capital of newer investors. These schemes lead you to believe that profits are coming from product sales or other means, while in reality, they're dependent on an ever-increasing flow of new investors.

- Fraudulent Exchanges: Some platforms may pose as legitimate exchanges to lure users into depositing funds, which are then stolen. These fake exchanges might offer features that sound too good to be true or may have very little to no user feedback.

Red Flags

Recognizing the red flags can help you avoid falling victim to these scams. Be cautious of:

Guaranteed Returns: In the world of investing, there are no guaranteed returns. Any promise of guaranteed profits should be treated as a major red flag.

Unsolicited Offers and High-Pressure Tactics: Be wary of unexpected offers, especially those that pressure you to make a quick decision.

Scammers often create a sense of urgency to push you into making decisions without due diligence.

Lack of Transparency: Genuine projects are transparent about their processes and who their team members are. A lack of clear information about the project's team, location, or how it works should raise suspicions.

Preventive Measures

To safeguard yourself against these dangers, consider the following preventive measures:

- Verify Legitimacy: Always check the credibility of the platforms or ICOs. Look for reviews, user feedback, and news articles. Visit forums like Reddit or BitcoinTalk, where the community discusses new projects.

- Use Two-Factor Authentication (2FA): Adding an extra layer of security can protect your accounts even if your password is compromised.

- Conduct Thorough Research: Before investing, research thoroughly. Check multiple sources and make sure you understand how the investment works. If the project is genuine, there will be plenty of verifiable information available.

Resources for Verification

To help you verify the credibility of crypto projects and offers, utilize resources such as:

- Blockchain Explorers: Tools like Etherscan or Blockchain.com allow you to track transaction histories and wallet balances, helping you verify the claims made by investment projects.

- Reputable Crypto News Websites: Websites like CoinDesk, CoinTelegraph, and CryptoSlate offer up-to-date news on the cryptocurrency world and can be a reliable source of information on new projects and potential scams.

- Regulatory Announcements: Keep an eye on announcements from financial regulators about new rules or warnings regarding cryptocurrencies and ICOs.

Visual Element: Checklist for Avoiding Crypto Scams

To simplify the process of identifying and avoiding scams, here's a handy checklist that you can refer to whenever you encounter a new investment opportunity:

1. Verify the URL: Ensure the website link is correct and not a close imitation of a well-known site.

2. Look for Secure Connections: Check for 'https' in the web address—a sign of a secure connection.

3. Research the Team: Look for clear information about the project team and their credentials.

4. Read the Whitepaper: Every legitimate project should have a detailed whitepaper. Read it thoroughly.

5. Check Token Economics: Understand how the tokens are distributed and what controls inflation.

6. Seek Community Feedback: Explore forums and social media to see what others are saying about the project.

This checklist can serve as a quick reference to ensure you're conducting the necessary due diligence before committing your funds to any crypto project. Remember, in the world of cryptocurrency, being well-informed is your best defense against scams. By taking proactive steps to verify the information and understand the investments you are considering, you can navigate this dynamic space with confidence and security.

The Importance of Regulatory Compliance in Crypto

Attempting to understand the global regulatory landscape for cryptocurrencies is akin to navigating a complex maze—each turn representing different national laws and international guidelines that directly impact how you engage in crypto trading and investment. Across the globe, the regulatory approach to cryptocurrencies varies widely; some countries embrace them, others regulate them heavily, and a few even ban them outright. For instance, in the United States, cryptocurrencies are treated both as commodities by the Commodity Futures Trading Commission (CFTC) and as property for tax purposes by the IRS. On the other hand, countries like Japan have acknowledged Bitcoin and other digital currencies as legal property and have a relatively straightforward regulatory framework that governs their trade. Conversely, China has taken a much stricter stance by banning all cryptocurrency exchanges and Initial Coin Offerings (ICOs) within its borders.

The impact of these regulations on investors cannot be overstated. Compliance with local and international regulations not only helps in avoiding legal pitfalls but can also significantly protect investors from fraud. Regulations require exchanges and ICOs to implement stringent security measures, conduct thorough audits, and maintain transparent operations. These regulations work to stabilize the crypto market by reducing fraud and increasing investor confidence. For instance, when exchanges comply with Anti-Money Laundering (AML) and Know Your Customer (KYC) regulations, it ensures that the platforms are not being used for illegal activities like money laundering. This compliance protects investors by ensuring that the platforms are safe and reputable, thereby safeguarding investor funds.

Navigating this complex regulatory environment requires a proactive approach. Start by educating yourself on the regulations that apply in your country and any other regions where you intend to trade. This knowledge is crucial as it directly affects how you report taxes, the legality of your transactions, and the types of crypto-related activities you can legally participate in. For US residents, this means understanding the reporting requirements set by the IRS regarding gains made from cryptocurrency transactions. In the European Union, you'll need to be aware of the Fifth Anti-Money Laundering Directive (5AMLD), which includes stricter transparency requirements.

Staying updated with regulatory changes is equally crucial. The world of cryptocurrency is fast-paced, with new technological advancements and regulatory changes occurring regularly. Subscribe to newsletters from regulatory bodies such as the Securities and Exchange Commission (SEC) in the US or the Financial Conduct Authority (FCA) in the UK. Following trusted crypto regulatory analysts on social media or professional networking sites like

LinkedIn can also provide timely updates and expert insights into how new regulations could affect your investment strategy.

Moreover, for international traders, understanding the global regulatory landscape is essential. The G20 countries, for example, have been working towards creating a unified framework that addresses the issues of crypto-assets. Being aware of such developments can help you anticipate changes in your home country's regulations and prepare accordingly.

Navigating compliance might seem daunting, but it is a fundamental aspect of engaging with cryptocurrencies safely and successfully. By understanding and adhering to the regulations, you not only protect yourself from legal repercussions but also contribute to the legitimacy and stability of the broader crypto market. Your proactive efforts in staying informed and compliant not only safeguard your investments but also enhance your credibility and reputation in the crypto community. As the regulatory landscape continues to evolve, your ongoing commitment to compliance will remain a cornerstone of your successful engagement with the world of cryptocurrency.

What to Do If You Suspect a Crypto Scam

Imagine you're browsing through your emails or scrolling through a social media feed, and you stumble upon an offer or an investment opportunity that seems a bit off. Maybe the promises seem too good to be true, or perhaps there's an unexpected urgency to act. You may have just encountered a crypto scam. Knowing what to do next can not only potentially save you from financial loss but also contribute to a safer crypto community by helping to expose fraudulent schemes.

The first step if you suspect a scam is to disconnect immediately. If you're on a website, close it; if you're in an app, exit. Do not click on any more links, and definitely do not provide any personal information or make any payments. If you've already shared some data or made a transaction, it's crucial to secure your assets next. Move your funds to a new wallet with a strong and unique password. If you suspect your financial information has been compromised, alert your bank or credit card company immediately to place holds on your accounts.

After you've secured your assets, it's time to report the scam. This is vital because timely reporting can help authorities catch the perpetrators and prevent them from harming others. Start by documenting everything about the scam, including emails, website links, social media posts, and any communications. Screenshots and URLs are particularly useful. Then, report the scam to the relevant authorities. In the United States, this could be the Federal Trade Commission (FTC) through their website or the Internet Crime Complaint Center (IC3). Many other countries have similar governmental bodies that handle fraud reports. Additionally, if the scam occurred on a social media platform or involved a specific cryptocurrency exchange, report the incident to those entities as well. Most platforms take these reports seriously and can take action to prevent further scams.

Seeking professional help is also a wise step, especially if significant assets are involved or if the scam has legal implications. A legal professional, particularly one with experience in fraud or cybercrime, can provide advice tailored to your specific situation. They can help you understand your rights and the possible recourse available to you. In some cases, they might even be able to help you recover lost funds. Additionally, consulting with a cybersecurity expert can help you secure your digital presence to prevent future incidents.

Finally, consider sharing your experience with the community. While it might feel uncomfortable to admit that you were targeted, publicly sharing your story can be incredibly beneficial to others. It raises awareness about the tactics scammers use and educates the public on how to recognize similar scams. You might opt to write a blog post, share an update on social media, or even speak at community events. Remember, every piece of shared knowledge contributes to a more informed and prepared community, making it harder for scammers to find victims.

Navigating through a suspected scam can be stressful and intimidating, but taking these steps will not only help to protect your assets but also contribute to the broader fight against cybercrime in the cryptocurrency space. By acting swiftly to disconnect and secure your assets, diligently reporting to authorities and platforms, seeking the right professional advice, and courageously sharing your experience, you play a crucial role in fortifying the defenses of the entire crypto community against fraudulent activities.

Risk Management Strategies for Crypto Investors

Navigating the cryptocurrency market effectively demands more than just knowing the best times to buy or sell. Having robust risk management strategies is like setting up guardrails on your investment journey—they don't obstruct the view but ensure you don't veer off the path during unexpected conditions. Let's explore some fundamental concepts and practical strategies in risk management that can safeguard your investments in the volatile world of cryptocurrency.

Fundamentals of Risk Management

Risk management in cryptocurrency investing involves identifying, assessing, and controlling threats to your capital. These risks can stem from market volatility, regulatory changes, technological failures, and security breaches, among other factors. Effective risk management starts with acknowledging that investments can go down as well as up, and some level of risk is always involved. Therefore, the goal is not to eliminate risk but to manage it intelligently to balance potential rewards with your tolerance for potential losses.

One fundamental concept here is the 'risk-reward ratio,' which investors use to compare the expected return of an investment with the amount of risk undertaken to capture this return. For instance, if you're eyeing a cryptocurrency with potentially high returns, it's crucial to assess whether the high volatility and possible losses are acceptable to you. Setting clear goals and knowing your financial threshold can help guide this decision-making process.

Diversification Strategies

Diversification is one of the most effective strategies used to manage investment risks. It involves spreading your investments across various asset types to reduce exposure to any single asset or risk. In the context of cryptocurrency, this could mean investing in different types of digital assets like Bitcoin, and Ethereum, altcoins with different functionalities, and even tokens from emerging sectors like DeFi (Decentralized Finance) or NFTs (Non-Fungible Tokens).

However, proper diversification also extends beyond crypto assets. Incorporating non-crypto investments like stocks, bonds, real estate, or commodities can provide a buffer against crypto market volatility. This blend of asset types tends to react differently to the same economic event, which can help stabilize your overall portfolio performance during market swings.

Utilizing Insurance Options

As the crypto ecosystem matures, more sophisticated risk management tools are becoming available, including insurance. Crypto insurance can protect against a variety of risks, including theft, hacking, and even the loss of access to your crypto due to forgotten passwords or failed hardware. Several companies now offer policies designed specifically for digital assets.

Choosing the right insurance policy involves understanding what's covered and what's not. Most policies cover the theft of digital assets up to a certain limit and under specific conditions. It's essential to work with insurers who understand the nuances of cryptocurrency and can provide policies that match your investment profile. Always read the terms carefully and consider whether the premium costs are justified by the coverage provided.

Building a Risk-Aware Culture

Maintaining a risk-aware culture is essential, especially in a field as young and rapidly evolving as cryptocurrency. This involves staying educated about market developments, understanding the technologies behind your investments, and staying alert to changes in the regulatory landscape that could affect your holdings.

Continuous education is critical, whether it's through reading up on new technologies, participating in community discussions, or following thought leaders and experts in the field. The more informed you are, the better equipped you'll be to make decisions that align with both market conditions and your personal investment goals.

By integrating these risk management strategies—understanding fundamental principles, diversifying your portfolio, utilizing insurance options, and fostering a risk-aware culture—you can navigate the crypto markets more safely and confidently. These strategies not only protect your investments but also give you a firmer foundation for exploring new opportunities in the dynamic world of cryptocurrency.

As we close this chapter, remember that managing risk is not about avoiding it but understanding and controlling it to your advantage. The strategies discussed here are tools to help you build resilience against the uncertainties of the market. In the next chapter, we'll shift our focus to advanced investment strategies that can further enhance your ability to capitalize on market opportunities while managing risk effectively.

Chapter 5

Beyond Basic Investments

The world of cryptocurrency offers a landscape ripe with opportunities for those willing to explore beyond the traditional pathways of buying and trading digital currencies. One of the most captivating developments in this dynamic field is the emergence of Non-Fungible Tokens or NFTs. Imagine owning a digital piece of art that, unlike any print or replica, is uniquely yours or holding a virtual real estate property in a digital world. This isn't a futuristic fantasy; it's a reality made possible by NFTs, transforming how we perceive ownership and value in the digital age.

Introduction to NFTs: Buying, Selling, and Trading

Understanding NFTs

Non-Fungible Tokens (NFTs) are digital assets that denote ownership of unique items or content, using blockchain technology to certify authenticity and ownership. Unlike cryptocurrencies like Ethereum or Bitcoin, which are fungible, this means that each unit is the same as every other unit; each NFT is unique, has distinct properties, and isn't interchangeable. This uniqueness is what gives NFTs their value, particularly in realms like digital art, collectibles, and virtual real estate. For instance, an NFT could represent an original digital painting, a one-of-a-kind virtual trading card, or an exclusive piece of virtual land in a blockchain-based online world.

How to Buy and Sell NFTs

The process of buying and selling NFTs typically takes place on specialized platforms that act somewhat like digital art galleries or collectible marketplaces. Some of the most popular platforms include Foundation, OpenSea, and Rarible. Here's how you can start your journey into the world of NFTs:

1. Set Up a Digital Wallet: You will need a digital wallet before you can trade NFTs: one that supports Ethereum, as most NFT platforms are built on the Ethereum blockchain. This wallet will be used to store your NFTs and process transactions.

2. Choose a Platform: Select an NFT marketplace that aligns with the type of digital asset you're interested in. Each platform has its own set of rules and fees and caters to different types of NFTs.

3. Create or Buy NFTs: If you're an artist or creator, you can perfect your own NFTs on these platforms, turning your digital art or collectibles into purchasable assets. If you're looking to buy, you can browse the marketplace for NFTs that catch your eye and purchase them using cryptocurrency.

4. Consider Transaction Fees: Be aware of the fees involved. Most NFT transactions require a 'gas' fee, which is a payment made to compensate for the computing energy required to process and validate transactions on the blockchain.

Market Trends and Valuation

The valuation of NFTs can be influenced by various factors, from the fame of the creator and the uniqueness of the content to the potential for future appreciation and the overall demand within the NFT market. For instance, an NFT created by a well-known digital artist may command a higher price than one by an emerging artist. Similarly, an NFT representing a key plot in a popular virtual world might be more valuable than a more common offering.

It's crucial to closely watch market trends. Platforms like NonFungible.com provide valuable data on market trends, sales, and average prices, helping you make informed decisions. Whether you're buying for personal enjoyment or investment potential, understanding these dynamics can enhance your ability to choose wisely and invest effectively.

Risks and Legal Considerations

While the NFT market offers exciting opportunities, it also comes with its share of risks and legal complexities. Market volatility is a significant factor; the value of NFTs can fluctuate wildly based on market trends and consumer interest. Additionally, copyright and ownership issues can pose legal challenges. It's crucial to verify the authenticity and copyright status of an NFT before purchasing. Ensure that the token you're buying genuinely represents the ownership rights it claims, and be aware of the legal implications, especially if you plan to reproduce or monetize the NFT.

Understanding these aspects of NFTs—from the basic functioning and trading process to the nuanced dynamics of market valuation and legal considerations—can equip you with the knowledge to navigate this innovative field. As you delve into the world of NFTs, remember to approach with curiosity and caution, balancing the allure of unique digital assets with a sound understanding of their value and risks.

Visual Element: Infographic on Steps to Buy and Sell NFTs

To help you visualize the process, here's an infographic that breaks down the steps to buying and selling NFTs. This visual guide provides a quick reference to ensure you have the essential information at your fingertips, simplifying your entry into the NFT market. Whether you're an artist looking to mint your first digital creation or a collector eager to explore unique digital assets, this guide aids in navigating the exciting realm of NFTs with confidence and ease.

Decentralized Finance (DeFi): An Emerging Frontier

Imagine a financial system where every transaction, agreement, and operation is transparent, easily accessible by anyone in the world, and operates without the need for traditional banks or financial intermediaries. That's the revolutionary promise of Decentralized Finance, commonly referred to as DeFi. Built on blockchain technology, particularly Ethereum, DeFi offers a global, open alternative to every financial service you use today—from savings, loans, and trading to insurance—and allows them to operate independently and more efficiently. This system isn't just for the tech-savvy or the financially privileged; it's designed to be accessible to anyone with an internet connection, fundamentally changing how we think about and interact with money.

DeFi uses smart contracts, which are self-executing contracts with the terms of the agreement directly written into the lines of code. These contracts operate on public blockchains, making them accessible to everyone but also irreversible and secure. These features form the backbone of various DeFi applications that aim to replicate and improve upon the services offered by traditional financial institutions.

Core DeFi Applications

One of the most common applications of DeFi is lending platforms. Platforms like Aave or Compound allow users to lend out their cryptocurrencies, like lending out money in a savings account, to earn interest directly from the borrower. What makes DeFi lending different is that it's entirely over-collateralized, meaning the borrower must lock up a higher amount of cryptocurrency than the amount they are borrowing. This collateral can be liquidated by the platform to pay back the lenders if the borrowers fail to uphold their side of the deal.

Another cornerstone of DeFi is decentralized exchanges (DEXs). Unlike traditional exchanges, DEXs allow users to trade cryptocurrencies directly without needing an intermediary to hold their funds. Platforms like Uniswap or SushiSwap use smart contracts to create liquidity pools that automatically execute trades based on pre-set algorithms. This not only speeds up the trading process but also increases security, as the tokens remain within the users' control, held by smart contracts rather than by the exchange.

Yield farming, a newer application, involves users moving their cryptocurrencies around between different lending and trading platforms to maximize their returns from DeFi lending and trading opportunities. It's akin to moving money between various bank accounts to take advantage of the best interest rates available, but it's executed in a way that's automated and can interact with multiple platforms at once.

Participating in DeFi

Getting involved in DeFi starts with setting up a digital wallet that will support Ethereum, such as MetaMask, Trust Wallet, or Coinbase

Wallet. These wallets not only store your cryptocurrency but also interact with DeFi applications directly through their interfaces. Once you've set up your wallet, you can connect it to a DeFi platform by visiting the platform's website and linking your wallet.

When you start interacting with DeFi platforms, you'll encounter transaction fees known as gas fees, which are payments made in compensation for the computing energy used to process and authenticate transactions on the Ethereum network. These fees will vary based on network demand and can become relatively high during peak times, so it's crucial to consider these costs when you're making transactions.

Security Practices in DeFi

While DeFi opens up enormous opportunities, it also comes with its set of risks, primarily technical risks from smart contract vulnerabilities. Smart contracts are only as secure as the code they are written with, and if there are bugs in the code, it can lead to funds being lost or stolen. Therefore, it's important to engage only with platforms that have undergone rigorous security audits by reputable firms.

It's also wise to diversify your DeFi interactions and not lock all your funds in a single platform or contract. Just as you wouldn't invest all your money in a single stock, you shouldn't expose all your digital assets to the risks of one single DeFi project.

The world of DeFi is still in its infancy but is rapidly evolving, continuously enhancing its protocols to offer more secure and effective financial services. By ensuring you understand the platforms and the technologies behind them, you can take advantage of what DeFi has to offer while mitigating the risks involved. Whether you're looking to earn interest on your crypto assets, borrow funds, trade tokens, or explore new financial products, DeFi provides a powerful, accessible set of tools that reimagines the future of finance.

Staking Cryptocurrencies: Passive Income Explained

In the evolving landscape of cryptocurrency investment opportunities, staking emerges as a compelling method to not only support the operational and security mechanisms of blockchain networks but also to earn rewards. Simply put, staking involves holding funds in a cryptocurrency wallet to support the operations of a blockchain network, and, in return, you receive a reward, much like interest in a traditional bank savings account. This process is particularly associated with cryptocurrencies that use the Proof of Stake (PoS) model. Unlike the energy-intensive Proof of Work (PoW) model used by Bitcoin, which requires computational power to mine new coins, PoS relies on participants holding stakes in the coin to validate transactions and create new blocks.

The allure of staking lies in its dual benefit: contributing to the blockchain's efficacy and security and earning potential passive income through staking rewards. However, the process and profitability of staking can vary significantly based on the cryptocurrency and the staking method chosen. Let's delve deeper into how you can engage with staking, the different approaches available, and the considerations you should keep in mind to optimize your staking strategy.

Choosing a Staking Option

Staking can be approached in several ways, each with its nuances. Direct staking involves participating directly in the blockchain by holding and offering your coins directly from your wallet. This method often requires meeting a minimum number of coins and running a node, which can be technical and may not be suitable for everyone.

Staking pools, on the other hand, are a more accessible option. They involve pooling your coins with other investors to increase your chances of validating blocks and earning rewards. Staking pools are managed by third parties and reduce the technical barriers associated with setting up nodes, making them a popular choice for individuals who may not have enough coins to meet the minimum requirements for direct staking or the technical expertise to run a node.

Third-party staking services offered by some cryptocurrency exchanges allow you to stake your coins directly through the platform. While this method offers convenience, it often comes with fees and somewhat less control over your staked assets. It's crucial to choose reputable services if you opt for this method, as the security of your staked assets depends on the platform's robustness.

There are pros and cons to each staking method. Direct staking gives you complete control and potentially higher rewards, but it's technically challenging and has higher entry requirements. Staking pools offer simplicity and lower entry barriers but may come with pool fees and slightly lower rewards due to distribution among more participants. Third-party services provide convenience but at the cost of control and potential platform risks.

Risks Involved in Staking

While staking offers numerous benefits, it's not without risks. Liquidity issues can arise, as staked coins are locked up and cannot be sold or moved until the end of the staking period, which might prevent you from accessing your assets quickly in volatile markets. Slashing is another risk, particularly in direct staking scenarios, where validators can lose a portion of their staked coins if they fail to validate blocks correctly or attempt to corrupt the network.

Additionally, the responsibility of running a node, if you are staking directly, includes ensuring your node is always online and functioning correctly, as downtime can also lead to penalties or reduced rewards. These risks necessitate a careful approach to staking. Ensuring regular updates and maintenance of your hardware and software, choosing reputable staking pools or platforms, and staying informed about the staking protocol and network conditions can help mitigate these risks.

Expected Returns

The potential returns from staking can be attractive, but they vary widely depending on the coin, the amount staked, network conditions, and the inflation rate of the staked asset. Generally, staking rewards can range from a modest 5% to an impressive 20% annual return, sometimes even higher. However, these returns are not guaranteed and can fluctuate based on the factors mentioned above. To set realistic expectations, it's advisable to research historical returns, understand the specific staking requirements and reward mechanisms of the blockchain you're interested in, and also consider the potential impact of market volatility on the value of your staked coins.

Staking stands out as a relatively accessible means of earning passive income while participating in the cryptocurrency ecosystem. It allows you to support the security and operability of blockchain networks while potentially growing your digital assets. Whether you choose direct staking, join a staking pool, or use a third-party service, understanding the intricacies of each method and the associated risks is crucial. With careful consideration and strategic planning, this can be a valuable addition to your cryptocurrency investment portfolio, aligning the growth of your assets with the advancement of blockchain technology.

Crypto Crowdfunding: Participating in ICOs Safely

In the bustling universe of cryptocurrency, Initial Coin Offerings (ICOs) represent a fascinating frontier of opportunity for both creators and investors. Much like a traditional IPO gives investors a chance to buy shares in a company, an ICO is a mechanism through which new crypto projects raise capital by issuing their own digital tokens to early backers. This form of crowdfunding is fueled by blockchain technology, which ensures the transparency and safety of transactions. Unlike traditional fundraising methods, where investors receive shares of a company, ICO participants are usually motivated by the potential utility of the token in the ecosystem being developed or by the prospect of the token gaining value over time.

Understanding the mechanics of ICOs is crucial before you decide to participate. Typically, a startup lays out its project in a whitepaper, including the technical details, the need for the token, how the funds raised will be used, and the overall goals of the project. Once the campaign commences, investors can buy the newly issued tokens with existing digital currencies, often Ethereum or Bitcoin. The allure of ICOs lies in the potential high returns. Early contributors to successful projects like Ethereum or NEO reaped enormous profits. However, the risks are equally significant due to factors like lack of regulation, potential for fraud, and high volatility.

Evaluating ICOs requires a meticulous approach. Start by assessing the credibility of the team behind the project. Research their past experience, their expertise in blockchain technology, and any history of successful projects. The feasibility of the project is another critical area to scrutinize. Understand the technology being proposed and whether it solves a real problem in a way that is achievable and sustainable. Tokenomics, or the economic model of the token, is also vital. Look at the total supply of tokens, the distribution plan, how the tokens will be used within the platform, and what gives the token its value.

Community engagement is an often underestimated aspect of a successful ICO. A strong, active community provides a foundation of support and advocacy for the project. Check social media platforms, Reddit, Telegram, and other forums where project discussions occur. The enthusiasm and engagement level of the community can provide insights into the potential success of the ICO.

Participating in an ICO involves several crucial steps to ensure you do so safely. Conducting thorough due diligence is the first step. This includes reading the project's whitepaper, understanding the legal implications, especially those concerning your jurisdiction, and researching all available information about the project and its team. Once you decide to proceed, you'll need to set up a digital wallet that supports the ICO's token. Make sure it's a wallet for which you control the private keys. Participating directly from an exchange is a common mistake that can lead to you losing your investment.

During the ICO, be vigilant and avoid phishing scams by double-checking all addresses and using official websites only. After acquiring your tokens, the safest practice is to move them to your private wallet, away from exchanges or platforms susceptible to hacks.

Post-ICO strategies involve careful monitoring and management of your investment. Deciding when to hold or sell the tokens can significantly impact your returns. This decision should be based on a thorough market analysis, project updates, and the overall performance of the crypto market. Staying informed through project updates, news sites, and community discussions is crucial. Many projects continue evolving post-ICO, and regulatory changes can also affect your holdings.

Navigating the ICO landscape can be thrilling and potentially rewarding if you are equipped with the proper knowledge and tools. By understanding how ICOs work, evaluating them critically, participating cautiously, and managing your investment wisely, you can engage with this innovative funding mechanism while mitigating the risks involved. Remember, in the volatile world of cryptocurrencies, staying informed and vigilant is your best strategy for success.

Exploring Crypto Derivatives: Options and Futures

Stepping into the realm of cryptocurrency derivatives might sound complex, but it's essentially about strategies that seasoned investors use to optimize their potential gains or hedge against possible losses. Derivatives in the cryptocurrency context involve contracts based on the future value of digital currencies. Two of the most common forms are options and futures. Options allow you to purchase or sell an asset at a predetermined price before a certain expiration date. On the other hand, futures are similar but come with the obligation to purchase or sell that asset at a set price on a specific future date.

Understanding how these instruments work is crucial for anyone looking to dive deeper into the financial mechanics of the crypto world. Trading crypto derivatives involves speculation on the price movements of cryptocurrencies without actually owning them. This is done through contracts that derive their value from the performance of an underlying asset, which, in this case, is a digital currency. The allure of derivatives trading lies in its ability to amplify gains through leverage. This leverage allows traders to gain a larger exposure to the market by using smaller upfront capital, known as margin. However, while leverage can magnify profits, it also increases possible losses, making it a double-edged sword.

Derivative trading platforms like BitMEX, Binance Futures, and Deribit facilitate these transactions. When you engage in a futures contract, for instance, you agree to buy or sell a specific amount of cryptocurrency at a predetermined price on a set future date. The actual mechanics involve various strategies and orders, such as long and short positions, which professional traders use to bet on whether the cryptocurrency will rise or fall. A long position indicates a bet on the price going up, while a short position bets on it going down.

The stakes in derivative trading are high, and so are the risks. The unpredictable nature of cryptocurrencies means prices can swing wildly, impacting derivatives even more due to their leveraged nature. If the market moves against your position, you could lose more than your initial investment, leading to a 'margin call' where you must add more funds to maintain your position or be forced to close it at a loss.

However, the potential rewards can be substantial. Skilled traders use derivatives to hedge other investments or to take advantage of market movements to turn a profit, even in a falling market. For instance, if you hold Bitcoin and think the price will drop temporarily, you might take a short position in Bitcoin futures to profit from this downturn, offsetting the losses in your actual Bitcoin holdings.

Best Practices for Engaging in Crypto Derivatives Trading

Navigating the high-risk world of crypto derivatives requires a well-thought-out strategy and adherence to best practices. First and foremost, educate yourself thoroughly. Understanding the underlying asset, how derivatives work, the specifics of contracts, and the platform you are using is fundamental. Many platforms offer demo accounts where you can practice trading without financial risk, which can be a valuable learning tool.

Choosing a reputable trading platform is crucial. Look for platforms with robust security measures, transparent fee structures, and solid reputations in the community. Since the regulatory landscape for crypto derivatives is still evolving, ensuring that the platform complies with relevant regulations is also essential to protect your investments.

Risk management is another critical area. Use risk management tools and strategies such as stop-loss orders, which automatically sell your contract at a predefined price to prevent significant losses. Diversifying your investments and not pouring all your capital into derivatives trading can also help manage risk.

Continuous learning is part of the journey. The cryptocurrency market is dynamic, with constant developments in technology, regulations, and market conditions. Staying informed through reliable news sources, ongoing education, and active community participation can help you adapt and make better trading decisions.

In conclusion, while the world of crypto derivatives offers exciting opportunities for gaining exposure to cryptocurrencies' price movements without owning them, it comes with high risks that require careful consideration and strategy. Whether you're looking to hedge your existing cryptocurrency holdings or speculate on future prices, understanding the complexities of options and futures is the key to navigating this advanced aspect of crypto investing successfully.

As we wrap up this exploration of advanced investment strategies in the world of cryptocurrency, remember that each instrument and approach we've discussed offers unique opportunities and challenges. From the transformative potential of NFTs and DeFi to the strategic applications of staking and derivatives, the landscape of crypto investing is rich with possibilities. Stay informed, stay cautious, and, as always, make sure your investment decisions align with your financial goals and risk tolerance.

Looking ahead, the next chapter will delve deeper into the evolving regulatory frameworks that shape the global cryptocurrency market, ensuring you're equipped to navigate not only the opportunities but also the complexities of this rapidly changing space.

Chapter 6

Advanced Market Analysis Techniques

Imagine you're a detective in the vast, bustling city of cryptocurrency markets, where every street corner, every shadow, holds clues to potential fortunes and pitfalls. Your tools? It's not just a magnifying glass but a whole arsenal of charts and technical indicators that help you decode the secrets hidden in plain sight. This is the world of technical analysis, a crucial skill for anyone looking to navigate the crypto markets not just with luck but with insight and precision. In this chapter, we'll dive deep into the art and science of reading charts, understanding market behaviors, and making informed predictions that could guide your investment decisions.

Technical Analysis: Reading and Understanding Charts

Chart Types and Setups

In the realm of market analysis, charts are like maps; they don't tell you where to go, but they show you the paths that have been taken before, helping you gauge where you might head next. Understanding different types of charts is foundational in technical analysis. Let's start with the basics: line charts, bar charts, and candlestick charts.

Line charts are the simplest form, plotting the closing price of an asset over a certain period. Imagine drawing a line through the daily closing prices of Bitcoin over a month; what you see is a line chart. It's straightforward and gives you a clear view of how the price has trended over time.

Bar charts take it a notch higher. Each bar represents trading action over a certain period, shows both opening and closing prices, and also the highs and lows. The bottom of the bar shows the lowest traded price for that period, and the top shows the highest price paid. This type of chart provides more data than a line chart and is particularly useful for seeing the volatility during each period.

Candlestick charts, originating from Japan over centuries ago, are arguably the most popular charting method in cryptocurrency trading. Each 'candle' provides four pieces of information: the opening price, the closing price, the high, and the low. What makes candlestick charts particularly valuable are the patterns they form, which traders use to predict price movement. For instance, a series of candles with small bodies but long wicks might suggest a reversal, or a 'doji' candle—where the open and close are virtually the same—can indicate indecision among traders about the asset's value.

Technical Indicators

While charts give you a visual representation of market behavior, technical indicators help by providing mathematical interpretations of market trends and cycles. Some of the most commonly used technical indicators include:

Moving Averages (MA) help smooth out price data by creating a constantly updated average price. The most common are the Simple

Moving Average (SMA) and the Exponential Moving Average (EMA). MAs can help identify a trend's direction and potential reversal points.

The Moving Average Convergence Divergence (MACD) is an indicator of momentum that follows trends and shows the relationship between two moving averages of a cryptocurrency's price. The MACD is calculated by subtracting the 26-period EMA from the 12-period EMA, which results in what is known as the MACD line. A signal line (the 9-period EMA of the MACD line) is plotted on the top of the MACD line and can then function as a trigger for buy and sell indicators.

Relative Strength Index (RSI) measures the speed and change of price movements. RSI oscillates between zero and 100. Traditionally, and according to Wilder, RSI is considered overbought when above 70 and oversold when below 30.

Fibonacci retracement levels are other powerful tools that are particularly interesting because they blend mathematics and art. They are founded on the idea that markets will retrace a foreseeable portion of a move, following which they will continue to move in the original direction. By identifying these retracement levels, you can better predict where the price might find support or resistance.

Chart Patterns and Trends

Recognizing patterns on these charts is like understanding the language of the markets. Some common patterns you should know include:

Head and Shoulders: This pattern, appearing at market tops, suggests a reversal of an uptrend and is one of the most reliable trend reversal patterns.

Flags and Pennants: These are continuation patterns where a sharp price movement is followed by a generally sideways price movement, which is then followed by a continuation of the prior trend.

Wedges: This pattern can signify either a continuance or reversal of a trend, depending on the direction of the wedge.

Integrating Multiple Indicators

The real skill in technical analysis comes not from using a single indicator but from integrating multiple tools to confirm trends and predict movements. For instance, you might use an RSI to identify whether an asset is overbought or oversold, then look for a confirming candlestick pattern and check Fibonacci levels for potential buy or sell points. This multi-layered approach can significantly enhance the reliability of your predictions..

In essence, diving deep into technical analysis equips you with the tools to not only survive in the crypto markets but to thrive. By understanding and utilizing these advanced techniques, you position yourself to make more informed decisions backed not just by gut feeling but by insightful interpretation of market data. As we continue to explore more complex aspects of market analysis in the following sections, keep these foundational tools in mind—they are the building blocks upon which successful trading strategies are built.

Fundamental Analysis of Cryptocurrencies

When you're considering investing in a cryptocurrency, it's like evaluating a tech startup. You wouldn't just look at the price of the company's stock; you'd consider what the company does, how it plans to succeed, and the people behind it. This is where fundamental analysis comes into play, a method extensively used in traditional finance and equally vital in the cryptocurrency world. Fundamental analysis in the context of cryptocurrencies involves assessing the intrinsic value of a digital asset by examining related economic, financial, and other qualitative and quantitative factors.

One of the first aspects to consider is the underlying technology of a cryptocurrency. What problem does this technology solve? How does it improve upon existing solutions? For example, Ethereum introduced smart contracts that automate transactions without any need for intermediaries, which opened up possibilities for numerous applications beyond simple transactions, like decentralized apps (dApps) and decentralized autonomous organizations (DAOs). Evaluating the technology involves understanding the blockchain's protocol, consensus mechanism, scalability, security features, and interoperability with other blockchains. Each of these factors can significantly impact the cryptocurrency's utility and market potential.

The use case of a cryptocurrency is another crucial element. It's essential to identify whether the token has a practical application that can drive demand beyond speculative trading. For instance, Binance Coin (BNB) started as a utility token offering reduced trading fees on the Binance exchange but rapidly expanded its use cases to payments for transaction fees on Binance's chain, token sales, and more. The broader and more robust the use case, the more likely the cryptocurrency will be demanded, which in turn supports its long-term value.

Market potential is about understanding the size of the market or industry the cryptocurrency aims to disrupt or enhance. For example, a cryptocurrency that seeks to streamline cross-border payments in the remittance market, which is worth billions of dollars, may have significant growth potential. Analyzing market potential involves researching the industry size, competitors, and the cryptocurrency's adoption rate within the market.

Importance of the Development Team and Community Support

The team behind a cryptocurrency can be a make-or-break factor in its success. A strong, transparent, and experienced team is often a good indicator of a project's potential. Look into the team members' backgrounds: Have they been involved in other successful projects? Do they have expertise in blockchain and the specific industry the cryptocurrency targets? For example, Vitalik Buterin, co-founder of Ethereum, was already well-known in the cryptocurrency community for his work before launching Ethereum, which helped garner initial support and credibility.

Community support also plays a critical role. Cryptocurrencies with active, engaged communities often see greater innovation and quicker adoption as community members contribute to the development, spread awareness, and use of the cryptocurrency. The size and engagement of the community can often be gauged through social media, cryptocurrency forums, and participation in blockchain events. A vibrant community not only helps in polishing the project through feedback and suggestions but also acts as a vital promotional tool that can drive adoption and increase the cryptocurrency's visibility.

Reading White Papers and Roadmaps

The white paper is a cryptocurrency project's blueprint; it outlines what the project aims to achieve, the technology behind it, the market potential, and more. Reading and critically analyzing a white paper is essential. Look for clarity and feasibility in its objectives, detailed and practical technological explanations, and a clear articulation of the use case. Also, assess the transparency of the white paper: does it cite sources, and does it provide realistic, transparent data to back its claims?

The development roadmap provides insights into the team's long-term vision and their commitment to achieving it. It should outline significant milestones and the timelines for achieving them. Frequent delays, overly ambitious timelines, or a lack of specific targets in the roadmap can be red flags, indicating poor planning or unrealistic goals.

Market and Competitive Analysis

Finally, understanding the competitive landscape is crucial. How does the cryptocurrency stand out from others with similar use cases? Analyzing its competitors involves looking at their market share, technological advantages, and community engagement. For instance, while assessing a new blockchain platform, compare its transaction speed, fees, and scalability to those of direct competitors like Ethereum and Binance Smart Chain.

This competitive analysis not only helps in understanding the strengths and weaknesses of the cryptocurrency you are considering but also in gauging its potential for growth and adoption in comparison to established players. This kind of analysis can provide a more comprehensive view of where the cryptocurrency stands and its potential to secure a niche within the competitive landscape.

By thoroughly applying fundamental analysis, you delve beyond the hype and headlines, equipping yourself with a deep understanding of what drives the value and potential of cryptocurrencies. This methodical approach allows you to make informed decisions, poised to identify opportunities where others might see mere fluctuations.

Sentiment Analysis: Gauging Market Emotions

In the fluctuating universe of cryptocurrency, understanding market sentiment is akin to feeling the pulse of the market. It's about gauging the emotional atmosphere among investors and traders, which can significantly influence price movements. Market sentiment reflects the overall attitude of the marketplace: are people feeling bullish (positive) or bearish (negative) about the future of a particular cryptocurrency? This sentiment can be a powerful yet sometimes elusive, indicator in the volatile crypto markets. Grasping it requires not only keen observation but also the right tools to sift through the vast amounts of data generated by market activities.

Tools and resources for sentiment analysis come in various forms, each offering a distinct slice of the market's emotional pie. Social media analysis, for instance, taps into the pulse of what's being discussed across platforms like Twitter, Reddit, and Facebook. By analyzing the frequency and tone of posts, tweets, and comments, you can get a sense of whether the sentiment towards a cryptocurrency is generally positive, negative, or neutral. Tools like Sentiment Analyzer or CryptoMood use natural language processing and machine learning to quantify this data, providing a more structured and quantifiable measure of social media sentiment.

Opinion polls and sentiment indicators also play crucial roles. Websites like Crypto Fear & Greed Index offer a daily sentiment score by analyzing different sources of data, including volatility, market momentum, and social media. This index, for example, tells you whether investors are feeling excessive fear, which might suggest a potential buying opportunity, or if the market is showing signs of greed, which could indicate a sell-off might be near.

Interpreting News and Media Influence

Understanding how to interpret news and media influence is crucial. The market in cryptocurrency is susceptible to news, which means it often reacts swiftly to announcements related to regulations, technological advancements, or financial results. However, not all news has a lasting impact on market sentiment, and distinguishing impactful news from mere noise is critical.

Impactful news typically involves fundamental changes or significant developments in the cryptocurrency ecosystem, such as a major country announcing new regulatory measures, significant technological breakthroughs, or major financial institutions adopting or investing in cryptocurrency. For example, when a large company like Tesla announced it had invested in Bitcoin and would accept it as payment, the market sentiment soared, driving up Bitcoin's price significantly.

On the other hand, the daily fluctuations of opinions and minor updates that don't affect the core aspects of a cryptocurrency might create noise—temporary ripples that might seem important but generally don't lead to long-term impact. Learning to differentiate between these can help you avoid reactionary decisions based on transient emotions and focus on news that substantiates potential long-term shifts in market dynamics.

Applying Sentiment Analysis

Incorporating sentiment analysis into your overall trading strategy can significantly enhance your decision-making process. It's about merging the emotional pulse of the market with more traditional technical and fundamental analyses to form a comprehensive view of the potential market movements.

For instance, if your technical analysis suggests that a cryptocurrency is about to break out, but sentiment analysis shows extreme fear in the market, it might be wise to tread cautiously. The market could be reacting to a recent piece of negative news, and despite what the technical indicators suggest, the price might drop instead of climb.

Using real-world examples, consider the impact of China's announcements on cryptocurrency regulations. Each time there was news about China tightening its stance on cryptocurrencies, the market typically reacted negatively, often resulting in significant price drops. Traders using sentiment analysis would have been on alert for such news and could have adjusted their trading strategies accordingly, potentially limiting losses or capitalizing on the buy-back opportunities these dips often present.

In essence, sentiment analysis offers a way to harness the emotional undercurrents of the market, providing you with insights that can help you anticipate and react to price changes more effectively. It's about adding another layer to your investment strategy, one that considers not just the numbers and trends but also the human emotions that drive market movements. By mastering this analysis, you position yourself to navigate the crypto markets not just with information but with insight into the collective mood of the market participants.

Leveraging Trading Bots: Do's and Don'ts

Imagine you had a tool that could handle the rapid and often exhausting demands of cryptocurrency trading for you, executing trades at optimal times, day or night, without your constant supervision. That's precisely what trading bots are designed to do. In essence, trading bots are software programs that will connect to a cryptocurrency exchange and make trades on your behalf based on predefined conditions. These bots can analyze market data, interpret it according to your strategy, and even make trading decisions that help maximize your profits—all without any direct input from you once they are set up.

When selecting a trading bot, several crucial factors come into play. Reliability is paramount; a bot that frequently goes offline or has software bugs can result in missed trading opportunities or even losses. Security is another primary consideration; the bot should have robust security measures to protect your investment, especially since it will have access to your exchange account. The user interface should be intuitive and user-friendly, allowing you to configure settings and understand features without needing a deep background in technology or trading. Lastly, cost is an important factor; some bots come with a subscription fee, while others might take a percentage of your profits.

Additionally, a solid community support system can be invaluable. A vibrant community can provide practical insights, strategies, and feedback that can help you get the most out of your trading bot. Developers who are transparent about their practices and offer regular updates can also be a sign of a trustworthy product.

Setting up a trading bot involves several steps, each important to ensure the bot functions correctly and aligns with your trading strategy. Initially, you need to choose a bot that fits your trading needs and is compatible with your chosen cryptocurrency exchange. Once selected, you'll typically download and install the software. Configuring your bot is the next critical step. This involves setting up trading strategies—the instructions that the bot follows when buying and selling on your behalf. These might include when to enter and exit trades, risk management rules, and what portion of your portfolio to trade. Many advanced bots offer backtesting features, which will allow you to test your strategy against historical market data before putting real money on the line. This can help refine your plan without any risk.

However, while trading bots can offer significant advantages, they also come with their own set of risks and ethical considerations. One of the primary concerns is market manipulation. Some unscrupulous traders might use bots to engage in practices like wash trading or pump-and-dump schemes, which are illegal and harmful to the market. It's crucial to use bots responsibly and ensure that your trading strategies don't inadvertently contribute to manipulative practices. Another risk is over-reliance on bots. Relying too heavily on automated systems can make you complacent about the nuances of the market and detached from your own trading decisions. It's essential to remain engaged and monitor your bot's performance, adjusting strategies as market conditions change.

In conclusion, when used wisely, trading bots can be powerful tools for automating trading strategies and maximizing your trading efficiency. By understanding and managing their associated risks and maintaining an active role in managing your strategies, you can leverage trading bots effectively while safeguarding your investments.

Cryptocurrency and Global Economic Indicators

In the interconnected world of finance, the waves of global economic indicators not only ripple through traditional markets such as commodities and stocks but also wash over the shores of the cryptocurrency landscape. Understanding how elements such as inflation rates, exchange rates, and economic policies influence cryptocurrency markets can offer you a nuanced perspective, enhancing your ability to make informed investment decisions.

Let's consider inflation rates, which reflect the rate at which the general level of prices for goods and services is rising and, subsequently, purchasing power is falling. Central banks attempt to limit inflation and avoid deflation in order to keep the economy running smoothly. Consider how Bitcoin has often been referred to as "digital gold," a potential hedge against inflation. This comparison stems from the cryptocurrency's designed scarcity, as there will only ever be 21 million bitcoins. When traditional currencies face inflation, meaning each unit of currency will purchase fewer goods and services, this scarcity can make Bitcoin more attractive, potentially driving up its price. Observing how cryptocurrencies react in countries experiencing high inflation rates can provide insights into future movements.

Exchange rates, the value of one currency for the purpose of conversion to another, also play a significant role. For instance, if the U.S. dollar strengthens against other currencies, it can make dollar-priced assets, including cryptocurrencies, more expensive for foreign investors, potentially reducing demand. Conversely, if the dollar weakens, those same assets become cheaper and more attractive to foreign investors, possibly pushing demand higher. Monitoring these trends can help predict inflows and outflows of capital into cryptocurrencies from abroad, offering strategic investment insights.

Furthermore, economic policies, particularly those related to monetary policy, can significantly impact cryptocurrency markets. Policies that increase money supply, typically lowering interest rates, can lead to lower returns on savings denominated in those currencies. This might make higher-risk assets, like cryptocurrencies, more appealing. Conversely, tightening monetary policies might make traditional investments more attractive, potentially decreasing investment in crypto assets. Understanding these relationships and their indicators can guide your crypto investment timing and strategy.

Cryptocurrencies as Economic Indicators

Interestingly, cryptocurrencies themselves are beginning to be viewed as economic indicators. Consider the relationship between Bitcoin prices and geopolitical tensions or economic instability. Often, in times of economic uncertainty, there's an observable increase in Bitcoin trading volumes and price, suggesting that some view and use cryptocurrencies as digital safe havens. Analyzing these movements can offer you insights into global economic sentiments and trends, further illustrating the intricate ties between traditional economic indicators and the relatively new crypto markets.

Correlation with Traditional Markets

Exploring the correlation between cryptocurrencies and traditional financial markets, such as stocks and commodities, can reveal fascinating insights into investor behavior and risk appetite. Historically, cryptocurrencies like Bitcoin have shown periods of both correlation and non-correlation with traditional markets. For instance, during times of market stress, such as the early months of the COVID-19 pandemic, both Bitcoin and stock markets saw significant drops, suggesting a temporary correlation likely due to investors seeking liquidity. However, there are also periods where cryptocurrencies have moved independently of traditional markets, highlighting their potential as diversification tools. Understanding these correlations and their exceptions can help in crafting a diversified investment portfolio that can better withstand market volatility.

Strategic Planning Using Economic Indicators

Incorporating global economic indicators into your cryptocurrency investment strategy involves scenario planning and hedging techniques. Scenario planning allows you to prepare for different future economic conditions, adjusting your investment strategy accordingly. For example, if you anticipate an economic downturn, you might increase your holdings in cryptocurrencies that have historically performed well as safe-haven assets. On the other hand, by hedging, using financial instruments or market strategies, you can offset the risk of adverse price movements, which is crucial. You might hedge your crypto investments by keeping a portion of your portfolio in fiat currencies or traditional assets like gold, which might behave differently under various economic scenarios.

By weaving these strategies into your investment approach, you can more adeptly navigate the complex interplay between global economic indicators and cryptocurrency markets. This not only enhances your ability to adapt to changing conditions but also positions you to capitalize on opportunities that others might miss.

As this chapter concludes, remember that the dance between cryptocurrencies and global economic indicators is nuanced and complex. By understanding this relationship, you're better equipped to make informed decisions, potentially leading to more robust investment outcomes. As we transition into the next chapter, we'll explore the regulatory frameworks shaping the global cryptocurrency landscape, an understanding of which is essential for every informed investor.

Chapter 7

The Intersection of Cryptocurrency and Technology

Imagine stepping into a world where your health records are as secure as the vaults of a bank, where every pill you take can be traced back to its origin, and where medical bureaucracy doesn't slow down the speed at which you receive care. This isn't a far-off fantasy; it's a reality being forged at the intersection of cryptocurrency and modern technology, particularly through the use of blockchain. In this chapter, we'll delve into how blockchain is revolutionizing the healthcare sector, enhancing data privacy, streamlining processes, and ensuring the authenticity of pharmaceuticals.

Blockchain in Healthcare: Improving Data Privacy

Securing Patient Data

In the realm of healthcare, patient data is both invaluable and incredibly sensitive. The security of this data is paramount, not just to maintain privacy but also to ensure trust in the healthcare system. Blockchain technology offers a potent solution by creating tamper-proof records of patient data. When information is added to a blockchain, it is encrypted and distributed across a network of computers, thereby making it nearly impossible to alter. Each block of data is linked to the one before it and after it, creating a chronological chain of records that is viewable by all parties but can only be updated through consensus among participants in the network.

This level of security means that sensitive information like your medical history, treatment plans, and prescription details are protected from unauthorized access and fraud. For you, this translates into peace of mind knowing your medical records are secure and only accessible to healthcare providers who have explicit permission to view them. Moreover, blockchain enables the secure sharing of your health data among authorized parties. Whether it's for consultation, diagnosis, or treatment, healthcare providers can access up-to-date, accurate information from anywhere in the world, facilitating better and faster care.

Streamlining Processes

The healthcare industry is notoriously bogged down by complex administrative processes, which can delay the delivery of care and lead to increased costs. Blockchain technology can streamline these processes by automating administrative tasks such as billing, claims processing, and compliance management. Smart contracts, which are self-executing contracts with the terms directly written into code, can automatically verify and process claims based on pre-set rules, significantly reducing the time and cost associated with manual processing.

For example, a blockchain system can automatically verify if a particular medical procedure is covered under a patient's insurance policy and then instantly process the claim, reducing the need for back-and-forth paperwork. This not only speeds up the processing of claims but also reduces the likelihood of errors and fraud, ensuring that healthcare providers are paid promptly and accurately for their services.

Enhancing Drug Traceability

The selling of counterfeit drugs is a significant issue in the pharmaceutical industry, posing serious risks to patient safety and costing the industry billions each year. Fortunately,   provides a robust solution to this problem through enhanced traceability of drug supply chains. Each step of a drug's journey from manufacturing to delivery can be recorded on a blockchain, creating a permanent history of the product's movement that can easily be traced back to its source.

This level of traceability ensures that you can be confident in the safety and authenticity of the medications you take. It also allows pharmaceutical companies to quickly trace and recall defective products, minimizing the impact of potential health risks.

Case Studies

Several healthcare organizations have already started to harness the power of blockchain to enhance data privacy and operational efficiency. For instance, a major hospital in the United States implemented a blockchain-based system to secure patient records and manage consent forms. The system allowed the hospital to easily manage and retrieve consent documents, ensuring compliance with healthcare regulations while providing patients with greater control over their personal information.

Another example is a global pharmaceutical company that used blockchain to track the distribution of medication in real time across multiple countries. This system helped the company combat counterfeiting and ensure that patients received genuine products.

These case studies demonstrate not only the practical applications of blockchain in healthcare but also its potential to fundamentally transform the industry, making it more secure, efficient, and patient-focused. As we continue to explore the intersection of cryptocurrency and technology, it becomes clear that the implications are vast, and the potential for positive change is enormous.

Smart Contracts: Transforming Legal and Business Processes

Smart contracts might sound high-tech and complex, but at their core, they're merely programs stored on a blockchain that run when predetermined conditions are met. They are digital contracts that automatically execute, control, or document legally relevant events and actions according to the terms agreed upon by the parties involved. Picture this: you're buying a house, and instead of going through heaps of paperwork, waiting for approvals, and dealing with intermediaries, you use a smart contract. This contract could automatically ensure that when you transfer the payment, the digital title deed is transferred to you. No middlemen, no extra fees, and no delays.

The advantages of smart contracts extend beyond just making transactions quicker. They can drastically reduce transaction costs because they cut out middlemen like brokers and lawyers, whose services can be costly. Additionally, smart contracts are executed by the computer code itself, which can dramatically reduce any errors that can arise from manually filling out heaps of forms. Also, because records on blockchains are encrypted, they are highly secure. The transparency of having transactions recorded on a blockchain ensures that all parties can view contract changes and outcomes, reducing the potential for disputes and enhancing trust among parties.

Looking beyond cryptocurrencies, smart contracts have diverse applications across various industries, reshaping how businesses and legal processes are handled. For example, in real estate, smart contracts may be used to handle the transfer of property titles and automate payments, reducing the time and paperwork involved in real estate transactions. In supply chain management, these contracts can be used to track the production, shipment, and delivery of products in real time. They ensure that each step in the supply chain is recorded, and if a product fails to reach a checkpoint by a specific time, the contract can trigger alerts and even withhold payments until issues are resolved.

In the realm of intellectual property rights, smart contracts can automate royalty payments. For instance, every time a song is downloaded, or a book is purchased online, a smart contract can ensure that the artists or authors receive their royalties immediately. This not only ensures that artists are paid fairly but also speeds up the process that customarily involves a lot of paperwork and time.

However, while smart contracts offer numerous benefits, they are not without challenges. One of the main hurdles is the legal recognition of smart contracts as legitimate substitutes for traditional contracts. The law in many areas is still catching up with the technology, and in many jurisdictions, digital contracts are not yet recognized as legally binding. This poses a risk, especially in transactions involving large sums of money or significant assets.

Scalability is another issue. As more transactions are carried out on blockchain networks, the volume of data being processed can lead to congestion, slowing down transactions and increasing costs, which diminishes one of the fundamental advantages of using smart contracts. Furthermore, while smart contracts are secure, they are only as good as the code they are written with, as bugs in the code can lead to unintended consequences, including security vulnerabilities. These technical obstacles require ongoing attention and improvements in blockchain and smart contract technologies.

Despite these challenges, the potential of smart contracts to revolutionize legal and business processes is immense. As technology advances and more sectors recognize and adapt to these benefits, we can see a significant transformation in how contracts are executed and enforced. This could lead to a more efficient, transparent, and fair way of conducting transactions across many aspects of business and law.

The Impact of Cryptocurrency on Global Remittances

Reducing Transfer Costs

Imagine sending money to your family halfway across the world, and more of your hard-earned cash actually reaches them without being eaten up by hefty transaction fees. That's one of the transformative benefits cryptocurrencies bring to the table, especially in the context of global remittances. Traditional wire transfers and international banking typically involve multiple intermediaries, each taking a slice of the transaction as processing fees. Cryptocurrencies streamline this process by enabling direct peer-to-peer transactions without the need for these intermediaries, significantly reducing the costs involved.

This reduction in cost is not just marginal; it can mean the difference between a family in a developing country affording an extra week's worth of groceries or not. For instance, consider a typical bank transfer where transaction fees can range anywhere from 5% to as high as 20% of the amount being sent, depending on the countries involved. In contrast, the transaction fee for sending cryptocurrencies like Bitcoin or Ethereum might only be a few cents or a small percentage, regardless of the amount or the geographic locations of the sender and recipient.

The impact is profound in regions where a significant portion of the population relies on remittances from family members working abroad. Lower fees mean more money sent home can be spent on essential living expenses, education, or starting small businesses, potentially lifting communities out of poverty and stimulating local economies.

Increasing Speed and Accessibility

Beyond just reducing costs, cryptocurrencies can revolutionize how quickly money is transferred across borders. Traditional remittance pathways can be slow, sometimes requiring several days to process due to the checks and balances of intermediate banks and financial services. Cryptocurrencies operate on blockchain technology that allows for almost instantaneous transactions. This means that what used to take days can now happen in a matter of minutes or even seconds, regardless of where the sender and recipient are located.

This speed of transaction provides not just convenience but also security. The quicker the money is transferred, the less time there is for potential interference or fraud along the way. Moreover, the accessibility of cryptocurrencies is a game-changer for the unbanked or underbanked populations. A significant number of adults worldwide do not have access to traditional banking services, which excludes them from the global financial system and makes it particularly challenging and expensive to receive remittances through conventional means.

Cryptocurrencies can be accessed by anyone with a smartphone and an internet connection, both of which are increasingly widespread, even in developing countries. This accessibility means that remittances can reach more people directly and safely, contributing to financial inclusion and empowerment.

Risks and Regulatory Challenges

However, the use of cryptocurrencies in remittances is not without its challenges, as the instability of cryptocurrency prices can be a substantial risk. The value of cryptocurrencies can dramatically increase or decrease within a short period, which means the actual value received by the end recipient can vary unpredictably. This risk can be mitigated by converting cryptocurrencies to stablecoins—cryptocurrencies pegged to less volatile assets like the US dollar—or immediately converting the received cryptocurrency into local currency.

Regulatory uncertainty also poses a challenge. A cryptocurrency's legal status varies significantly from one country to another. In some places, it is still a grey area with ongoing debates about how to implement effective regulations without stifling innovation. These regulatory challenges can impact the legality and reliability of using cryptocurrencies for remittances. Staying informed about the regulatory environment and compliance requirements in both the sender's and recipient's countries is crucial for those considering cryptocurrencies for remittances.

Examples of Cryptocurrency Use in Remittances

Several countries and entities have successfully harnessed the power of cryptocurrencies to enhance their remittance systems. For example, in the Philippines, a country where remittances constitute a significant part of the GDP, several blockchain-based remittance services have emerged. These services leverage cryptocurrencies to facilitate faster and cheaper transfers for the millions of Filipinos working abroad. In Africa, companies like BitPesa use blockchain technology to help businesses in multiple countries pay their employees and suppliers in other parts of the world, reducing transfer costs and times dramatically.

These examples underscore the potential of cryptocurrencies to transform the remittance industry by making transfers faster, cheaper, and more accessible. As technology continues to evolve and regulatory frameworks become clearer, the role of cryptocurrencies in remittances is likely to grow, offering a lifeline to millions of individuals who depend on these funds for their livelihood.

Cryptocurrencies in the Gaming Industry

In the dynamic world of gaming, where fantasy realms and digital landscapes flourish, cryptocurrencies are making significant inroads, transforming how transactions are conducted and how players interact with virtual economies. Think of a gaming world where every purchase of armor or every trade of goods doesn't just rely on traditional in-game currency that holds no value outside the game but uses cryptocurrencies that carry real-world value. This integration not only enhances the gaming experience by adding a layer of authenticity and value to in-game economies but also revolutionizes the financial dynamics of gaming.

Cryptocurrencies facilitate transactions within these virtual worlds with a level of efficiency and security that traditional in-game currencies simply cannot match. By using blockchain technology, transactions are recorded on a decentralized ledger, ensuring transparency and reducing the chances of fraud. This setup allows for the seamless purchase of digital goods and services within the game, making the process smoother and more reliable. For gamers, this means the ability to buy, sell, and trade in-game assets without the usual hassles of conversion rates and transaction fees associated with standard currencies. It connects different gaming platforms and economies, making digital assets more liquid and, thus, more valuable.

Moreover, cryptocurrencies are dramatically changing how players interact with their virtual assets. Through blockchain technology, when you acquire an in-game item, it can actually be yours. This means that players have absolute ownership of their in-game assets, as each item can be uniquely identified and ownership verified on the blockchain. This ownership extends beyond the game itself, allowing players to trade or sell their assets on external markets, potentially earning real money. The implications are profound; items like unique swords, rare skins, or even characters can become collectibles, much like physical items in the real world. This shift not only makes gaming more engaging and potentially profitable for players but also ensures that their investments in time and money are tangible and protected.

For game developers, cryptocurrencies open up new avenues for monetization that go beyond traditional methods like advertisements or one-time in-app purchases. Through tokenization, where in-game assets are linked to crypto tokens, developers can create more immersive and financially sustainable ecosystems. Players might buy tokens to access special content or unique abilities, and because these tokens can also be traded outside the game, they remain valuable to players, driving engagement and retention. Additionally, developers can earn a commission on transactions happening in and out of the game, providing a continuous revenue stream that is not limited to initial sales or ads.

While the potential of cryptocurrencies in gaming is vast, integrating them into mainstream gaming platforms presents several challenges. Scalability is a major concern; as games attract millions of players worldwide, the underlying blockchain must be able to handle a vast number of transactions quickly and efficiently. Current technology still struggles with these demands, leading to potential delays and increased transaction costs, which could detract from the gaming experience.

User adoption also poses a significant hurdle. Despite the growing popularity of cryptocurrencies, many gamers are new to blockchain technology and may hesitate to embrace these new systems. Educating users and demonstrating the tangible benefits of using cryptocurrencies in gaming are crucial steps toward widespread adoption.

Speculating on future developments, as gaming platforms become more sophisticated and blockchain technology advances, the integration of cryptocurrencies in gaming could become more seamless. Innovations such as layer-two solutions or sidechains could address the issues of scalability by allowing transactions to occur off the main blockchain, speeding up processing times and reducing costs. As more gamers recognize the benefits of actual digital ownership and developers find innovative ways to incorporate token economies, cryptocurrencies could well become a standard element of the gaming industry, transforming how players and developers interact and creating a new paradigm for the digital gaming economy.

Blockchain for Social Good: Real-World Applications

When you think of blockchain, your mind might first jump to cryptocurrencies and financial transactions. However, the potential of blockchain extends far beyond this, playing a pivotal role in social change across the globe. One of the most significant impacts of blockchain is its capability to enhance trust and transparency, particularly within charitable organizations. Traditionally, when you donate to a charity, it can be challenging to track where your money actually goes or whether it's being used effectively. Blockchain introduces a layer of accountability and transparency that was previously difficult to achieve.

On a blockchain, every transaction is recorded on a public ledger, which is immutable. This means that once a record is made, it cannot be altered or deleted. For charitable organizations, this can revolutionize how donations are tracked and reported. Donors can see exactly where their funds are going and follow the money as it moves toward its intended projects. This transparency not only reassures donors but also discourages mismanagement of funds within the organizations. For example, a blockchain platform could be used to track the distribution of funds in real-time as they are passed from the charity to purchase supplies and then to their final destination in a relief effort. This kind of traceability can significantly boost the trust and credibility of charitable organizations, encouraging more people to donate and contribute to crucial causes.

Blockchain also holds transformative potential for empowering economically disadvantaged communities. One significant way it achieves this is through the provision of secure digital identities. Around the world, a shocking number of people do not have any form of official identification, which can prevent them from accessing essential services like banking, healthcare, and education. Blockchain technology can offer a secure, immutable form of digital ID that is recognized and accepted worldwide. With such an ID, individuals can open bank accounts, sign legal contracts, access government services, and more. Moreover, blockchain can facilitate microloans directly to individuals or small businesses, bypassing traditional banking barriers and high interest rates. This direct financial empowerment can be a game-changer for lifting communities out of poverty.

In terms of enhancing environmental sustainability, blockchain technology is being used innovatively to support efforts across the globe. One notable application is in the tracking of carbon credits. Carbon credits are permits that allow the holder to emit a certain amount of carbon dioxide or other greenhouse gases. The calculation, tracking, and exchange of these credits can be complex and opaque. Blockchain provides a tamper-proof, transparent system for managing carbon credits to ensure that they are only counted once and used correctly. Additionally, blockchain is being utilized to verify the sustainability of supply chains. For instance, it can track the journey of a product from a sustainably managed forest through processing and manufacturing all the way to the retail shelf. This not only helps to ensure compliance with environmental standards but also boosts consumer confidence in sustainable products.

Case Studies of Successful Implementations

Looking at real-world examples, the World Food Programme (WFP) has successfully implemented blockchain technology to aid in the distribution of assistance to refugees. Their 'Building Blocks' project uses blockchain to make cash transfers more efficient, secure, and transparent. This initiative has helped to significantly reduce payment costs, increase data security, and ensure that aid reaches its intended recipients without any diversion.

Another compelling case is that of BitGive, the first Bitcoin nonprofit recognized by the IRS. BitGive has developed a platform called GiveTrack, which uses blockchain to allow donors to trace their donations. Donors can track how funds are spent, see the outcomes of their donations, and even communicate with the beneficiaries. This level of transparency and engagement increases the trust and satisfaction of donors, potentially leading to more substantial and sustained contributions.

These cases highlight just a few ways blockchain is being used to foster transparency, empower individuals, and address complex environmental issues. By leveraging this technology, we can make significant strides toward a more equitable and sustainable world. As we continue to explore the vast potential of blockchain, it becomes increasingly clear that its impact extends well beyond the financial sector, offering promising solutions to some of the most pressing social challenges of our time.

Chapter 8

Cryptocurrency and Society

Imagine a world where your economic status or geographical location doesn't limit your access to financial resources. Where the simple click of a button could offer you the same financial services that someone in a bustling financial district enjoys. Cryptocurrency is not just digital money; it's a revolutionary tool that is leveling the financial playing field across the globe. Let's delve into understanding its pivotal role in enhancing financial inclusion, particularly for those previously sidelined by traditional banking systems.

The Role of Cryptocurrency in Financial Inclusion

Cryptocurrency emerges as a beacon of hope, especially for the unbanked and underbanked populations. Think about someone living in a remote village where the nearest bank could be miles away, requiring hours of travel. For such an individual, traditional banking isn't just inconvenient; it's practically inaccessible. Cryptocurrencies are changing this narrative by providing financial services through mobile phones—a technology increasingly widespread even in remote areas. This aspect of digital currencies is not just about convenience but about offering fundamental financial services: saving money, receiving loans, and ensuring direct payments for work, which are crucial for daily survival and economic advancement.

The barriers to entry in the traditional banking world—documentation requirements, minimum balance stipulations, and sometimes discriminatory practices—often exclude low-income individuals and those without a fixed address. Cryptocurrencies dismantle these barriers. They operate on technology that allows anyone with a smartphone and internet access to create a wallet without any minimum balance or the bureaucratic red tape associated with traditional bank accounts. This inclusivity opens a world of opportunities for millions who were previously part of the cash-only economy, susceptible to theft and loss.

Empowering Microtransactions and Microfinance

One of the most transformative aspects regarding emerging markets of cryptocurrencies is their ability to facilitate microtransactions and microfinance. These are crucial for small-scale entrepreneurs who might need small amounts of capital to start or expand their businesses but are unable to secure loans from traditional banks due to a lack of collateral or credit history. Cryptocurrencies enable transactions that are not just secure and fast but also incredibly low in cost, allowing for the profitable transfer of tiny amounts of money. This capability is vital for microentrepreneurs looking to grow their businesses one small step at a time.

Moreover, the divisibility and portability of cryptocurrencies mean that these transactions can occur anywhere, eliminating the geographical constraints that often hinder traditional banking. A craftsman in a small village can receive a microloan from a lender in a metropolitan city, or a farmer can buy seeds using a fraction of a Bitcoin or Ethereum without needing physical cash or going through a bank.

Case Studies of Cryptocurrency in Emerging Markets

Let's consider a few real-world implementations that highlight the impact of cryptocurrencies on financial inclusion. In Kenya, the introduction of BitPesa has allowed users to send and receive money across borders more cheaply and quickly than traditional banks would allow. BitPesa uses Bitcoin as a medium for transferring funds, significantly lowering the cost of transactions and enabling East Africans to do business with companies around the world without needing a bank account.

In Venezuela, amidst hyperinflation and economic instability, cryptocurrencies have provided an alternative means of storing value that's more stable than the local currency. Platforms like Dash have become popular because they offer not only an opportunity for savings but also for transactions, allowing users to pay for daily expenses such as groceries and medicine with cryptocurrency. This shift has been crucial in helping individuals and businesses survive in an economy where the national currency has failed.

These examples underscore the profound impact cryptocurrencies are having on financial inclusion, demonstrating their potential to empower economically marginalized communities. By providing an alternative to traditional monetary systems, cryptocurrencies are not just changing how people transact; they are fundamentally altering the economic landscape, offering more people the opportunity to participate in the global economy on fairer terms. As we continue to explore the intersection of cryptocurrency and society, it's clear that the potential of these digital assets extends far beyond mere financial speculation; they are powerful tools for social and economic empowerment, paving the way for a more inclusive global financial system.

Privacy and Anonymity in Cryptocurrencies

When you think about privacy in financial transactions, what comes to mind might be a sealed envelope or a private meeting room. In the digital world, achieving this level of confidentiality is complex, especially with traditional financial systems that inherently require some level of personal disclosure. Enter privacy-focused cryptocurrencies like Monero and Zcash, which provide a digital equivalent of that sealed envelope, ensuring that your financial transactions remain confidential and untraceable. These cryptocurrencies use sophisticated cryptographic techniques to shield transaction details, including the identity of the sender and receiver, as well as the amount being transferred, from being publicly accessible on the blockchain.

Monero, for example, utilizes something called ring signatures and stealth addresses. Ring signatures mix a user's account keys with public keys from the blockchain to create a unique signature that can authenticate a transaction without revealing which specific keys were involved. This mechanism makes it extraordinarily difficult to trace the transaction back to any user. A stealth address adds another layer of privacy by creating a one-time address for each transaction so that all payments are received from unique addresses that cannot be linked to any previous transactions or to the receiver's primary address. Zcash uses a different approach known as zk-SNARKs (Zero-Knowledge Succinct Non-Interactive Arguments of Knowledge), which allows transactions to be verified without revealing any details about the transaction to the blockchain. This technology essentially allows for a transaction to be fully encrypted on the blockchain yet still considered valid and secure.

While these privacy features offer significant advantages for users seeking anonymity, they also bring forth complex legal and ethical considerations. Privacy coins are often scrutinized because their anonymity can potentially be exploited for illegal activities, including tax evasion, money laundering, and financing terrorism. This has led to debates about the balance between privacy rights and regulatory requirements. Regulatory bodies in several countries are grappling with creating frameworks that prevent illicit use without infringing on individual privacy rights. The challenge lies in implementing know-your-customer (KYC) and anti-money laundering (AML) laws in a way that does not completely strip away the anonymity features that define privacy coins.

Compared to traditional financial systems, where every transaction through a bank or credit card is traceable and tied to personal identities, cryptocurrencies offer a distinct advantage in terms of privacy. Traditional systems often involve extensive personal documentation and continuous tracking of financial activities, leaving a digital paper trail that is accessible to banks and, by extension, to government bodies. In contrast, transactions with privacy coins can occur without any personal information being disclosed, giving users control over their own financial privacy.

However, it's crucial to address common challenges and misconceptions associated with these cryptocurrencies. A significant challenge is the misconception that privacy in cryptocurrencies is absolute. While privacy coins enhance anonymity, they are not entirely untraceable. Advanced blockchain analysis techniques and network surveillance can sometimes lead to the de-anonymization of parties involved in transactions, especially if other operational security measures are not effectively implemented by the users. Moreover, the misconception that privacy coins are primarily used for illicit activities can overshadow their legitimate uses, such as protecting individuals living under oppressive regimes or safeguarding sensitive transactions in business dealings.

Understanding the nuances of privacy in cryptocurrencies involves recognizing what these technologies can and cannot do. While they offer enhanced privacy compared to traditional financial transactions, they are not a foolproof solution to all privacy concerns. As the technology evolves and regulatory landscapes adjust, the conversation around privacy coins will likely continue to grow, highlighting the ongoing need to balance privacy rights with security and regulatory requirements.

The Environmental Impact of Cryptocurrency Mining

When you hear about cryptocurrency mining, you might imagine complex algorithms and digital coins popping out of the ether. However, the real picture involves massive computational power and, consequently, significant energy consumption, especially for cryptocurrencies that operate on a proof-of-work (PoW) system. PoW, used by Bitcoin and many other cryptocurrencies, requires miners to solve complex mathematical problems to validate transactions and secure the network. This process, known as mining, is energy-intensive because it involves numerous computers competing to solve these problems first, thereby earning the right to add a new transaction block to the blockchain.

The energy consumption of these mining operations is staggering. For instance, Bitcoin's annual energy consumption is comparable to that of entire countries like Sweden or Malaysia. This immense energy use primarily stems from the electricity needed to power the high-performance computers that miners use. Much of this energy comes from power plants that burn fossil fuels, which contributes significantly to carbon emissions, a leading cause of global warming. Moreover, the electronic waste produced by cryptocurrency mining is a growing concern. As mining hardware becomes obsolete, it creates a stream of electronic waste that is difficult to recycle, given the specialized nature of these devices.

Beyond the carbon footprint, large-scale mining operations can also have more direct impacts on the environment. In regions where cryptocurrency mining is prevalent, the demand for electricity can lead to increased strain on local power grids, which can cause power shortages and increase the reliance on environmentally harmful backup power sources like diesel generators. Additionally, the heat generated by extensive mining farms can contribute to local temperature increases, affecting local climates and wildlife.

Despite these challenges, the cryptocurrency community is increasingly aware of the environmental impacts and is taking steps toward more sustainable practices. Innovations and initiatives aimed at reducing the environmental footprint of cryptocurrency mining are on the rise. One significant shift is the move towards using renewable energy sources to power mining operations. Solar, wind, and hydroelectric power are becoming more popular among miners, especially in regions where these resources are abundant and cheap. For example, some mining farms in Scandinavia take advantage of cheap hydroelectric power and a cool climate to reduce the energy consumption and cooling needs of mining operations.

Another promising development is the shift towards less energy-intensive consensus algorithms like proof-of-stake (PoS). Unlike PoW, PoS does not necessitate miners to solve intricate mathematical problems. Instead, validators are selected to create new blocks based on the number of coins they hold and are willing to use as collateral. This method not only reduces the amount of power needed to maintain the network but also incentivizes the holding of coins, which can lead to a more stable cryptocurrency environment. Ethereum is the second-largest cryptocurrency by market capitalization and is in the process of transitioning from PoW to PoS. This move is expected to decrease its energy consumption by up to 99%.

Globally, the regulatory response to the environmental impact of cryptocurrency mining has been varied. Some countries have embraced the challenge, implementing regulations and providing incentives for cleaner mining practices. For instance, Iceland has become a hub for sustainable cryptocurrency mining due to its abundance of renewable energy sources and natural cooling environments. Meanwhile, other countries have taken a more stringent approach. China, once home to over two-thirds of the world's cryptocurrency mining, has banned the practice entirely in some regions, citing excessive energy consumption and environmental concerns.

These examples illustrate the complex interplay between innovation, regulation, and environmental responsibility in the realm of cryptocurrency mining. As the industry continues to evolve, the push for sustainable development could not only alleviate the environmental impact of digital currencies but also lead to broader applications of eco-friendly technology in other sectors. By staying informed and supporting sustainable practices, you can contribute to this vital transition, ensuring that the future of finance does not come at the expense of the planet's health.

Cryptocurrency and Cybersecurity: What You Need to Know

Navigating the digital seas of cryptocurrency not only offers vast opportunities but also brings its own set of risks, particularly in cybersecurity. As you dive deeper into this world, understanding these risks and knowing how to protect yourself are crucial.

Common threats like exchange hacks, wallet breaches, and phishing attacks can turn what should be an exciting venture into a nightmare. Imagine logging in to find your digital wallet has been emptied or your personal information has been compromised. These scenarios are not just hypothetical; they happen more often than you might think.

Exchange hacks have been some of the most high-profile security breaches, with attackers stealing millions of dollars worth of cryptocurrencies. These platforms are prime targets due to the large amounts of assets they hold. Similarly, wallet breaches occur when unauthorized users gain access to a cryptocurrency wallet, enabling them to transfer funds. Often, this can be due to weak security practices like the use of simple passwords or storing information in easily accessible places. Phishing attacks, perhaps the most insidious, involve tricking individuals into giving away sensitive information, such as login credentials or private keys, often through fake websites or misleading emails that appear to be from legitimate sources.

Preventing such incidents begins with adhering to best practices for security. One of the most effective measures you can take is the use of hardware wallets to store your cryptocurrencies. Think of a hardware wallet as a personal safe—only much more compact and portable. Unlike online wallets or those hosted on mobile devices or computers, hardware wallets store your private keys offline on a physical device that can resemble a USB stick. This method, known as 'cold storage,' significantly reduces the risk of your funds being accessed via the Internet. Additionally, maintaining robust security on your physical device is crucial; this includes setting up strong, unique passwords and considering additional security measures like biometric locks.

Moreover, multi-factor authentication (MFA) adds an extra layer of security, but bear in mind that MFA requires more than one method of verification before access is granted; typically, it is something you know (like a password), something you have (like a smartphone to receive a code), and something you are (like a fingerprint or facial recognition). Implementing MFA can make unauthorized access considerably more difficult, providing an additional safeguard against hacking attempts.

The inherent features of blockchain technology also contribute significantly to enhancing cybersecurity. The decentralization of blockchain means that instead of being stored in a single central server, copies of the blockchain ledger are held on multiple computers across the globe. This distribution of data not only makes tampering with recorded transactions challenging but practically impossible without being noticed by other participants in the network. Moreover, the encryption used in blockchain adds another layer of security. Each transaction is securely linked to the one before and after it, and to alter any piece of information, one would need to alter all subsequent entries, which is computationally impractical.

As the cryptocurrency landscape continues to evolve, so too do the security challenges associated with it. One emerging threat is the potential impact of quantum computing. Quantum computers, which are still in the early stages of development, theoretically can process tasks at speeds unimaginable to current standards, potentially enabling them to break the cryptographic algorithms that currently protect blockchain transactions. This possibility suggests a future where blockchain technology may need to adapt to resist quantum attacks by upgrading to quantum-resistant cryptographic algorithms.

Another future challenge lies in the increasing sophistication of cyber-attacks. As technologies evolve, so do the tactics of cybercriminals, who continually develop new methods to exploit system vulnerabilities. The cryptocurrency community must stay vigilant, continuously updating and strengthening security measures. This includes regular software updates, audits, and the adoption of emerging technologies that enhance security.

Navigating the complexities of cybersecurity in the cryptocurrency world is no small feat. Yet, by understanding the common threats and adopting vigorous security measures, you can protect your digital assets and personal information effectively. As you continue to explore the vast possibilities that cryptocurrencies offer, remember that your security practices can significantly impact your success and safety in this digital frontier.

The Future of National and Digital Currencies

As we navigate through the evolving landscape of finance, one of the most significant developments we're witnessing is the adoption of digital currencies by central banks around the world. These central bank digital currencies (CBDCs) are state-controlled alternatives to traditional paper money and even decentralized cryptocurrencies like Bitcoin. Unlike their decentralized counterparts, CBDCs are not a scheme to escape governmental oversight; instead, they are an embodiment of it, offering nations a new tool to maintain financial sovereignty and improve monetary policies.

The development of CBDCs is gaining momentum, with countries like China testing the Digital Yuan and the European Central Bank exploring a Digital Euro. These digital currencies aim to offer the benefits of cryptocurrencies—speed, security, and digital transferability—while maintaining the regulated, stable value of traditional currencies. The potential impacts on the global financial system are profound. CBDCs could streamline cross-border transactions, reduce transaction costs, and provide an alternative to the U.S. dollar for global trade, which could alter international economic dynamics significantly.

Switching gears, let's consider the distinctions between decentralized cryptocurrencies and state-controlled digital currencies. The former operates on a distributed ledger technology without centralized control, which fundamentally challenges the traditional, centralized system of financial governance. This decentralization offers advantages such as reduced transaction fees and greater user autonomy but also comes with challenges like price volatility and regulatory issues. On the other hand, digital currencies controlled by states offer stability and are backed by governmental monetary policies, yet they raise concerns about privacy and the potential for governmental overreach in financial transactions.

The integration of both types of digital currencies into the traditional banking system is an unfolding story. We're beginning to see a hybrid approach where banks are exploring blockchain technology to enhance efficiencies and reduce costs. This integration is likely to expand further as regulatory frameworks around cryptocurrencies mature and technological solutions are developed to bridge the gap between different types of currencies. The future could see banks maintaining balances in both fiat and digital currencies, seamlessly operating in a dual-currency environment to meet the diverse needs of their customers.

Speculating on what the future holds, it's expected that technological advancements will continue to drive the evolution of both national and digital currencies. User adoption rates will play a crucial role in shaping this landscape. As more people become comfortable using digital currencies and as the technology becomes more integrated into everyday financial activities, we can expect these currencies to become a staple in financial portfolios. Moreover, global economic conditions—such as inflation rates, economic growth, and geopolitical tensions—will influence the pace and nature of this adoption.

In navigating this future, we are not just passive observers but active participants. The choices we make, whether as consumers, investors, or policymakers, will shape the trajectory of these technologies and their impact on our global financial system. As we wrap up this exploration of the future of national and digital currencies, we're reminded of the broader implications of our topic. We're not merely discussing currency evolution; we're looking at a potential redefinition of economic sovereignty and personal financial agency in the digital age.

Moving forward into the next chapter, we will delve deeper into the technologies that underpin these developments. Understanding these will not only enhance our grasp of the current landscape but also empower us to make informed decisions as we navigate the future of digital finance.

Chapter 9

Mastering Crypto Taxation and Legal Issues

Imagine you've just found a treasure chest, but instead of gold coins, it's filled with various cryptocurrencies. You're thrilled at first, but then reality sets in—how do you manage this newfound wealth responsibly, especially when it comes to taxes? Navigating the labyrinth of cryptocurrency taxation isn't as daunting as it might seem, and understanding it can save you from unnecessary headaches and maximize your investments. Let's break down the essentials of crypto taxes and regulations in the U.S., ensuring you stay compliant and informed.

Understanding Crypto Taxes and Regulations in the US

Cryptocurrencies, despite their digital nature, aren't free from the grasp of taxation. The IRS treats cryptocurrencies as property in the United States, not currency. This classification has significant implications for your tax liabilities. Every time you sell, trade, or use cryptocurrencies to purchase goods, you're potentially creating a taxable event. The IRS requires you to report these events, and failure to do so could lead to penalties or audits.

Taxable Events

Let's dive deeper into what constitutes a taxable event in the realm of cryptocurrency. The most common events include:

- Trading Crypto: Swapping one cryptocurrency for another is a taxable event, where you realize capital gains or losses based on the value differences between the traded assets.

- Spending Crypto: Using cryptocurrencies to purchase goods or services also triggers a capital gains tax, calculated from the difference between the price you acquired the asset and its value at the time of the transaction.

- Mining Crypto: If you're mining cryptocurrencies, the fair market value of the coins at the time of delivery will be considered as taxable income.

- Earning Crypto: Earning cryptocurrencies through services or as payment for goods also counts as taxable income, based on the value of the crypto at the time it was received.

Understanding these events is crucial for managing your tax obligations effectively. Each event has its nuances, and how you report them can significantly affect your tax outcomes.

State vs. Federal Regulations

While federal tax requirements are consistent across the U.S., state regulations can vary dramatically. Some states treat cryptocurrency transactions more favorably than others. For instance, certain states have exempted cryptocurrencies from state securities laws, making them more attractive to crypto investors and businesses. Conversely, others have stricter regulations that might complicate tax reporting or operational compliance. It's essential to be aware of the regulations specific to your state, ensuring you adhere to both federal and state tax laws.

Recent IRS Updates and Guidance

Keeping up-to-date with IRS guidelines is critical as the landscape of cryptocurrency taxation evolves. The IRS has been refining its policies to address the complexities and nuances of crypto transactions. Recent updates have clarified the reporting requirements for specific scenarios, such as hard forks, airdrops, and the tax treatment of staking rewards. These updates aim to provide clearer guidance for taxpayers, ensuring they understand their obligations and can report their transactions accurately.

For instance, the IRS's recent guidance on hard forks and airdrops clarifies that if new cryptocurrencies are created and you have control over them, their fair market value must be reported as ordinary income. This guidance is crucial for anyone involved in cryptocurrency activities, as it impacts how you assess and report your income.

Navigating the maze of cryptocurrency taxation might seem overwhelming at first, but with a proper understanding of the rules and regulations, you can manage your crypto assets wisely. Staying informed and compliant not only helps you avoid legal pitfalls but also empowers you to make the most of your investments in this dynamic digital landscape. Remember, knowledge is not just power in the world of cryptocurrency—it's profit.

How to Report Crypto on Your Taxes

When it comes to dealing with cryptocurrencies, whether you're a casual investor or an expert trader, one of the most vital aspects to keep on top of is how to report your crypto transactions on your taxes. The first step in this process is meticulous documentation.

Every transaction you make, from selling Bitcoin to using Ethereum to buy a coffee, needs to be recorded. You should note the date of each transaction, the amounts involved, the market value of the crypto at the time of the transaction, and any fees you paid. This might sound tedious, but it's crucial for accurate tax reporting. Each piece of data plays a critical role in determining your tax obligations and can help you minimize your tax liability legally.

Let's dive deeper into why each piece of information is important. The date of the transaction establishes when the tax liability is incurred, which is essential for calculating holding periods that determine whether gains are taxed as short-term or long-term. This can significantly affect the tax rate applied, as the amount and market value are necessary in calculating your gain or loss from each transaction. For instance, if you bought Bitcoin at $35,000 and sold it at $40,000, your gain would be $5,000, which is subject to capital gains tax. Transaction fees, while often overlooked, can also affect the cost basis of your crypto, potentially reducing the taxable gain when you sell it.

Moving onto the tax forms, if you've engaged in crypto transactions throughout the year, you'll likely need to familiarize yourself with IRS Form 8949 and Schedule D. Form 8949 is where you list all transactions involving capital assets, including cryptocurrencies. Here, you'll detail each transaction and report the date acquired, date sold, proceeds, cost basis, and gain or loss. Schedule D is used to summarize your total losses or capital gains reported on Form 8949. If you've just dabbled in crypto and only have a few transactions, this might seem straightforward. However, if you're a frequent trader or have numerous transactions, this can quickly become complex.

This complexity is why many turn to tax software and tools designed to handle cryptocurrency transactions. These tools can automatically import your transactions from various exchanges via API access or through transaction history files you upload. They then calculate your gains and losses, taking into account the dates and values of each transaction. Some popular options include CoinTracker, CryptoTrader, Tax, and ZenLedger, which offer a range of features, from simple gain and loss calculations to complete tax preparation services. However, they're not without limitations. Most require a subscription fee, and their accuracy depends heavily on the completeness of the transaction data they can access. If you've used multiple exchanges or have private transactions, ensuring the software has a complete record can be challenging.

Given the complexities and the potential for significant financial implications, many crypto investors choose to consult with a tax professional. This is especially advisable if you have a large volume of transactions, participate in activities like staking or mining, or if you receive airdrops or rewards. Tax professionals specializing in cryptocurrency can provide tailored advice that considers the latest tax laws and your specific situation. They can help ensure that you're taking advantage of all available tax strategies, such as identifying which cryptocurrencies to sell to optimize your tax liability based on holding periods and cost basis. They can also assist in situations where you might need to amend past returns due to incorrectly reported crypto transactions—a not uncommon scenario given the evolving nature of crypto tax guidance.

In essence, the process of documenting and reporting your cryptocurrency transactions for tax purposes, while potentially daunting, is a crucial aspect of managing your investments.

Thorough record-keeping, understanding which tax forms to use, utilizing robust tax software, and, when necessary, enlisting the help of a professional are all steps that will help you navigate the complexities of crypto taxation. With these practices in place, you can focus more on your investment strategies and less on administrative burdens, ensuring that you remain compliant while optimizing your financial outcomes.

Legal Challenges in Cryptocurrency Ownership and Transfer

When you hold cryptocurrencies, it's not just about keeping track of your digital assets; it's also about understanding the complex legal landscape that governs their ownership and transfer. One of the foundational aspects of owning cryptocurrency is grasping the concept of ownership rights and proof. Unlike traditional assets, where proof of ownership might involve a physical deed or a certificate, cryptocurrencies are entirely digital, and ownership is defined by who holds the private keys. These keys enable you to access and control your cryptocurrency. Therefore, maintaining the security of your private keys is paramount. Think of your private keys like the combination to a safe—except this safe holds your digital wealth. If you lose access to your private keys, you effectively lose ownership of your cryptocurrency with no way to retrieve it because there's no central authority or system to appeal to for recovery.

Moreover, the security of your digital assets doesn't just hinge on keeping your private keys safe from loss—it also involves safeguarding them from unauthorized access. This is where the legal aspect comes into play. If someone else gains access to them without your permission, the decentralized and anonymous nature of blockchain can make it nearly impossible to recover your assets.

This is why employing robust security measures, such as using hardware wallets to store your private keys offline, is crucial.

Additionally, understanding and using the technology correctly is critical to ensure that you do not inadvertently expose your private keys while transacting online.

Now, let's consider the complexities of smart contracts. These self-executing contracts have the terms written into code, then stored and replicated on the blockchain, and supervised by the computer network running the blockchain. This technology allows parties to transact securely and transparently without an intermediary. However, the enforceability of smart contracts under current law presents potential challenges, especially in dispute resolutions and contractual obligations. For instance, what happens if there's a bug in the code that executes a different transaction than agreed upon? Or if one party finds a way to exploit a loophole in the contract's code to their advantage? The decentralized nature of blockchain means there's no central authority to arbitrate such disputes, which could complicate legal proceedings.

Furthermore, as smart contracts are relatively new and the laws surrounding them are still developing, not all jurisdictions may recognize them as legally binding agreements.

This can lead to challenges in enforcing the terms of a smart contract in a court of law, should the need arise. As the use of smart contracts becomes more widespread, we can expect more legal frameworks to adapt and provide clearer guidelines on their usage. However, until then, parties using smart contracts should be cautious and consider seeking legal advice to understand the risks and how they might be mitigated.

Moving on to estate planning and inheritance, cryptocurrencies present unique challenges. Given their digital nature and the fact that they are not held in traditional bank accounts, they can be easily overlooked or forgotten after the owner's death. To prevent this, it's crucial to include your digital assets in your estate planning. This involves ensuring that detailed instructions about accessing your cryptocurrencies are available to your heirs without compromising the security of your private keys. Consider using a service that allows you to securely store your digital asset information in a way that it can only be accessed by your beneficiaries upon your death.

Finally, cross-border legal issues are another significant area of concern for cryptocurrency owners. Different countries have varied regulations regarding cryptocurrencies, which can affect everything from your ability to conduct transactions to your obligations for reporting for tax purposes. For instance, some countries may have strict capital controls that prohibit or limit the transfer of cryptocurrencies across borders or may apply different tax treatments to gains made from cryptocurrency transactions. Additionally, the global nature of cryptocurrencies and the potential for them to be used in international transactions can complicate compliance with international anti-money laundering (AML) and counter-terrorism financing (CTF) laws.

Navigating these complex legal challenges requires staying informed about the latest regulations in your area and any others you interact with. It also involves taking proactive steps to secure your assets and plan for the future. As the legal landscape around cryptocurrencies continues to evolve, staying adaptable and informed will be the key to successfully managing your digital assets.

International Crypto Laws: What Investors Should Know

Navigating the international landscape of cryptocurrency laws can often feel like trying to find your way through a labyrinth. Each country has its own set of rules and regulations, which can significantly affect your decisions and strategies as an investor. For instance, while some countries embrace cryptocurrencies with open arms and minimal regulation, others impose strict controls or outright bans. Understanding these differences is crucial for anyone involved in the international crypto market.

In the European Union, the regulatory environment is particularly complex due to the convergence of member states' laws with EU-wide regulations. A significant aspect of EU regulations that affect cryptocurrencies is the General Data Protection Regulation (GDPR), which imposes strict rules on the handling of personal data. Given that blockchains are inherently transparent and immutable, reconciling GDPR requirements with blockchain technology presents a unique challenge. For instance, the GDPR's "right to be forgotten," which allows individuals to request the deletion of personal data, seems at odds with the blockchain's permanent record-keeping. This discord has prompted ongoing discussions and developments within the EU to find a balanced approach that respects both privacy rights and the technological framework of cryptocurrencies.

Moreover, compliance with Anti-Money Laundering (AML) and Counter-Terrorism Financing (CTF) laws is a universal requirement across jurisdictions. These laws are designed to prevent illicit activities such as money laundering and terrorist financing, and they apply to cryptocurrency transactions just as they do to traditional financial transactions. Compliance involves performing due diligence on customers (often referred to as Know Your Customer or KYC procedures) by monitoring transactions for suspicious activities and reporting to regulatory bodies as necessary. The penalties for non-compliance can be severe, ranging from hefty fines to operational shutdowns, making it imperative for crypto businesses and investors to adhere strictly to these regulations.

Navigating tax obligations in the international arena can be particularly tricky. Each country has its own tax rules regarding cryptocurrencies, and these can vary widely. For example, some countries treat gains from cryptocurrencies as capital gains, while others might treat them as income, each with different tax implications. Furthermore, if you are a resident of one country but transact on an exchange based in another, you may be subject to tax obligations in both jurisdictions. Managing these obligations requires a careful understanding of the tax laws applicable to each transaction and jurisdiction. Strategies to manage potential tax liabilities include using accounting methods that optimize tax outcomes, such as choosing specific identification of coins sold to control which gains are realized.

Cryptocurrencies continue to gain popularity, so we can expect further developments in international regulations. Keeping abreast of changes is essential for anyone engaged in the global cryptocurrency market. Staying informed can help you navigate the complexities of international crypto laws, ensuring compliance and optimizing your investment strategy.

Reflecting on what we've covered in this chapter, it's clear that the landscape of crypto taxation and legal issues is both complex and dynamic. From understanding the intricacies of U.S. tax requirements to navigating the global regulatory environment, the need for diligent management and a proactive approach is evident. As we move forward, the intersection of technology, law, and finance will likely continue to evolve, presenting both challenges and opportunities. By staying informed and adaptable, you can navigate these waters successfully, ensuring compliance while maximizing your investment potential.

As we close this chapter on the legal and tax intricacies of cryptocurrencies, we turn our attention to the future. The next chapter will explore emerging trends and technologies in the crypto space. We'll look at what's on the horizon for digital currencies and blockchain technology, preparing you to navigate and leverage these advancements effectively.

Chapter 10

Staying Ahead in the Crypto World

Imagine the crypto world as a vast, ever-changing landscape, where today's lush valley might be tomorrow's mountain peak—or vice versa. Staying ahead in this dynamic environment isn't just about keeping up; it's about actively engaging with the continuous flow of information and learning. In this chapter, we'll explore how you can maintain your edge by developing a robust learning routine, diversifying your educational resources, making wise use of social media, and connecting with the community through conferences and meetups.

Keeping Up with Crypto: Best Practices for Continuous Learning

Establishing a Learning Routine

Your journey through the crypto world can be thrilling, but without a map and a compass, it's easy to lose your way. Establishing a learning routine is like setting up a navigation system that keeps you on the right path. This routine should include daily or weekly habits such as reading leading crypto news websites to ensure you're up to date with market trends and technological advancements. Websites like CoinDesk, Cointelegraph, and CryptoSlate offer timely and detailed articles that cover everything from market analysis to regulatory news.

Additionally, tuning into updates from influential crypto analysts and thought leaders can provide deeper insights and diverse perspectives that help refine your understanding and strategies. Podcasts and YouTube channels, such as "Unchained" by Laura Shin or "The Pomp Podcast" by Anthony Pompliano, feature interviews with industry experts and discussions on complex topics made accessible. Regularly monitoring these sources will not only keep you informed but also enhance your ability to anticipate market movements and make informed decisions.

Engaging with Educational Content

While staying updated on the news is crucial, deepening your knowledge through structured learning is equally important. The crypto and blockchain space is rich with educational content that ranges from books and online courses to webinars and workshops. For example, enrolling in courses offered by platforms like Coursera, Udemy, or the CryptoCurrency Certification Consortium (C4) can provide you with a structured and comprehensive understanding of various aspects of blockchain technology and cryptocurrency investing.

Diversifying your learning resources ensures that you're not only getting a wide range of information but also accessing multiple teaching styles that can help reinforce your learning. For instance, attending webinars and interactive workshops not only provides visual and auditory learning but also allows you to ask questions and engage in discussions, thereby enhancing your understanding and retention of information.

Using Social Media Wisely

Social media platforms, such as Reddit, Twitter, and LinkedIn, are treasure troves of information and community engagement—if used wisely. They offer real-time updates, trending discussions, and direct interactions with leaders and enthusiasts in the crypto space. To make the most out of social media, follow reputable accounts of crypto analysts, influencers, and news outlets. Engage in communities like r/CryptoCurrency or LinkedIn groups dedicated to blockchain technology to exchange ideas and get diverse opinions.

However, the key is to remain critical of the information you consume. The open nature of social media allows for a mix of insightful content and misinformation. Always cross-reference news and tips with credible sources and avoid making investment decisions based exclusively on social media trends. Being selective and thoughtful about your sources on these platforms can turn them into valuable tools for learning and networking.

Attending Crypto Conferences and Meetups

Nothing beats the immersive experience of attending crypto conferences and meetups. These events are not just about listening to talks but also about engaging with a community of like-minded individuals who are equally passionate about the future of cryptocurrencies. Conferences like Consensus or the North American Bitcoin Conference bring together industry leaders, innovators, and investors and provide a wealth of knowledge and networking opportunities.

Meetups in your local area can be found on platforms like Meetup. com, offering more frequent and accessible opportunities to connect with local crypto enthusiasts. These gatherings can be invaluable for sharing experiences, discussing strategies, and even forming partnerships. The benefits of attending these events extend beyond just gaining knowledge; they also embed you within a community that can support and inspire you as you navigate the complex world of cryptocurrency.

By integrating these practices into your routine, you are not only staying informed but also actively participating in the crypto community. This proactive approach to learning and engagement will provide you with the knowledge and connections to thrive in the ever-evolving cryptocurrency landscape.

Participating in Crypto Communities and Forums

Engaging with online communities and forums dedicated to cryptocurrency can transform your understanding and approach to investing. These platforms are more than just spaces for discussion — they are vibrant ecosystems where novices and experts alike converge to share insights, strategies, and firsthand experiences. Selecting the right communities is crucial; you want to be part of groups that are not only active but also informative. Cryptocurrency forums, Discord servers, and specialized Telegram groups are excellent starting points. Look for communities that foster a culture of helpfulness and are known for their knowledgeable members. The quality of discourse can significantly vary, so it's beneficial to spend some time lurking in these groups to gauge the depth and relevance of the discussions before fully engaging.

Once you've found communities that resonate with your needs, understanding and adhering to netiquette — internet etiquette — is vital. Every community has its set of rules, often explicitly stated, but there's also an unwritten code of conduct based on respect and constructive communication. For instance, it's good practice to search the forum before posting questions to avoid duplicates, which clutter the platform and can frustrate regular users. Engage respectfully, appreciating that behind every username is a person who might be more or less knowledgeable than you are. Constructive disagreement over different investment strategies or interpretations of market behavior is beneficial; it exposes you to new perspectives and deepens your understanding. However, these discussions should always be conducted respectfully and without personal attacks.

Active participation in these communities is not just about taking in information but also contributing to discussions. Start by responding to others' posts with thoughtful comments or insightful questions. Once you feel more confident, initiate discussions or share articles that you find compelling and think might help others. This proactive engagement is beneficial for several reasons. Firstly, it enables you to clarify your own thoughts and refine your strategies by articulating them to others. Secondly, it builds your reputation in the community, opening up more opportunities for deeper engagement and networking. Over time, you might find yourself in conversations with thought leaders or seasoned investors whose advice could be instrumental in shaping your investment approaches.

Learning from community experiences is perhaps one of the most valuable aspects of participating in crypto forums and groups. Members often share their successes and, more importantly, their mistakes. These narratives are goldmines of practical advice, offering unfiltered insights into the realities of cryptocurrency investment and security practices. For example, a common discussion might revolve around the pitfalls of failing to secure one's digital wallet or falling prey to phishing scams. These stories provide real-life lessons on what to do and what not to do, serving as both warnings and educational tools. By understanding and internalizing these experiences, you can avoid common errors and make informed decisions in your crypto ventures.

Moreover, some of the most enlightening moments in these forums come from collaborative problem-solving. When members encounter complex challenges or unique scenarios, the collective expertise of the community can come together to provide solutions and ideas that no individual might have considered. This collaborative environment not only helps solve individual issues but also contributes to the collective knowledge base, enhancing the overall sophistication and savviness of the community.

In essence, engaging with the right crypto communities and forums can significantly enhance your learning curve and improve your effectiveness as a crypto investor or enthusiast. By choosing active and informative platforms, respecting community etiquette, actively contributing to discussions, and learning from collective experiences, you can gain a wealth of knowledge and insights that are rarely found in textbooks or traditional courses. These interactions provide a dynamic learning environment that keeps pace with the swiftly evolving world of cryptocurrency, preparing you to navigate its complexities with greater confidence and competence.

Future Trends: What Next for Cryptocurrencies?

As we look toward the horizon of the cryptocurrency sector, it's clear that the landscape is poised for significant evolution, driven by advancements in technology and shifts in regulatory and environmental paradigms. One of the most compelling technological frontiers is quantum computing. Unlike traditional computing, which uses bits as the smallest unit of data, quantum computing uses qubits. This allows them to perform complex calculations at speeds unattainable by current standards, potentially decrypting algorithms that keep cryptocurrencies like Bitcoin secure. While this poses a risk, it also catalyzes the crypto community to innovate on quantum-resistant blockchain technologies, ensuring that your digital assets remain safe against even the most cutting-edge adversarial technologies.

In parallel, Artificial Intelligence (AI) integration is set to redefine how blockchain operates. AI can optimize mining processes, enhance security protocols, and even make autonomous trading decisions. By analyzing vast amounts of data and recognizing patterns faster than any human, AI systems could potentially predict market trends and provide investors with incredibly accurate insights. This integration could lead to smarter, more efficient blockchain networks that are both more secure and more profitable for those who understand how to leverage these AI capabilities.

Furthermore, scalability remains a critical challenge for blockchain technology. The Lightning Network for Bitcoin is a second-layer solution and offers promising remedies. These protocols operate on top of a blockchain to enable faster transactions and better scalability by handling transactions off the main chain while still maintaining security and decentralization. This could mean that in the future, you could use cryptocurrencies for everyday purchases, such as coffee or groceries, without experiencing delays and high transaction fees, making digital currencies more practical for everyday use by mainstream consumers.

Predicting market movements has always been part of the crypto investor's toolkit, but with the advent of algorithmic trading and predictive analytics, this process is becoming more sophisticated. Algorithmic trading uses mathematical models to make transaction decisions, executing orders at speeds and frequencies that are challenging for human traders. When combined with predictive analytics, which uses real-time and historical data to predict future market trends, investors can make more informed decisions. These tools are becoming increasingly accessible to the average investor, leveling the playing field between institutional investors and individual traders.

On the regulatory front, the landscape is continually evolving. As cryptocurrencies gain popularity, governments around the world are beginning to recognize the need for regulation to mitigate risks such as fraud, money laundering, and market manipulation. However, there's a delicate balance to strike. Over-regulation could stifle innovation and the growth of cryptocurrencies, while under-regulation could lead to investor harm and financial instability. Future regulatory frameworks will likely focus on enhancing transparency, improving security standards, and protecting investors, all while ensuring that the innovative spirit of the crypto world remains unhindered.

Lastly, the sustainability of cryptocurrency operations is becoming a priority. The traditional model of crypto mining is energy-intensive, contributing to carbon emissions and environmental degradation. However, the industry is shifting towards more sustainable practices, including the use of renewable energy sources such as solar, wind, and hydroelectric power. Innovations like green blockchain technologies and energy-efficient consensus algorithms like Proof of Stake (PoS) are gaining traction. These developments are not just good for the planet; they also offer a more sustainable path forward for the growth of cryptocurrencies, ensuring that the digital asset space can continue to expand without contributing disproportionately to environmental issues.

These emerging trends and technologies herald a transformative phase in the cryptocurrency sector, promising to make digital currencies more secure, efficient, and integrated into everyday financial activities. As these advancements unfold, staying informed and adaptable will be vital in successfully navigating the future landscape of cryptocurrencies.

Investing in Crypto Startups: Risks and Rewards

Investing in crypto startups is akin to planting seeds in a garden that's still being mapped out; it's filled with potential but requires patience, nurturing, and a deep understanding of the landscape to thrive. When you're looking to invest in these burgeoning companies, the first step is evaluating their viability. This isn't just about checking their current market performance or funding rounds; it involves a deeper analysis of their business models, the specific needs they aim to meet within the market, their technological innovations, and the expertise of their team.

Start by examining the business model of the crypto startup. What problem is it solving, and how does it intend to solve it? Is there an obvious demand for this solution in the crypto market? These questions help you gauge the practicality and potential longevity of the startup. For instance, a crypto venture that aims to enhance blockchain scalability is addressing a clear, existing issue that could improve how systems operate, indicating a strong market need. Next, look at the technology itself—is it innovative, and more importantly, is it feasible? Cutting-edge technology that's not practical or is too ahead of its time might not achieve commercial success. Lastly, a competent and experienced team is crucial. The presence of skilled professionals who have navigated similar arenas or have a strong track record in tech and business leadership is often a promising sign that they can steer the startup toward success.

The avenues for investing in crypto startups are diverse, each carrying its unique flavor of risk and potential reward. The sale of tokens, also known as Initial Coin Offerings (ICOs), is widespread. This allows startups to raise capital and issue their own digital currency, which can be used on their platform or traded on crypto exchanges. While ICOs can offer high returns, they are also risky, especially if the tokens don't gain market traction or the project fails to develop as promised. Equity investments are another pathway, where you buy a share of the company itself, giving you a potentially stable investment tied to the company's overall success and a vote in major decisions. Crowdfunding platforms represent a more accessible option, allowing you to invest smaller amounts in various startups, spreading your risks while still supporting innovative projects.

When diving into startup investments, managing risk is paramount. Diversification is critical—spread your investments across various sectors within the crypto world, such as mining, blockchain development, or financial services, to mitigate risks associated with any single area. Setting clear investment goals and understanding your own risk tolerance can guide your investment choices, helping you decide how much to invest and when to exit. Legal implications are also critical; ensure you understand the regulatory environment as it can impact startup operations and your rights as an investor.

Exploring case studies of both successful and failed crypto startups can provide invaluable lessons. Take the example of a successful startup like Binance, which grew from an ICO to a significant global digital currency exchange. Key factors in its success included addressing a clear market need for more secure and efficient crypto trading platforms, a strong leadership team, and robust technology. On the flip side, consider the cautionary tale of BitConnect, a platform that promised high returns on investment through its trading bot but was ultimately shut down after being accused of creating a Ponzi scheme. This case highlights the importance of due diligence and the risks of high-yield investment promises in the crypto space.

By understanding these dynamics, you can better navigate the exciting yet complex terrain of crypto startup investments, making informed decisions that align with your financial goals and risk tolerance. Engaging with this emerging market offers the dual thrill of potential financial reward and the opportunity to be part of innovative projects that could shape the future of technology. As you consider your next steps, remember that, like any investment, clarity, strategy, and continuous learning are your best tools for success.

Leveraging Augmented Reality for Cryptocurrency Learning

Augmented Reality (AR) is a technology that overlays digital information onto the real world, enhancing your perception of reality through devices like smartphones or AR glasses. This fusion of digital and real-world elements creates engaging and interactive experiences that can transform educational methods, especially in complex fields like cryptocurrency. By integrating AR into crypto education, learners can visualize and interact with abstract concepts such as blockchain operations, cryptocurrency mining, and trading processes in a more tangible way, making these topics more accessible and easier to understand.

The application of AR in crypto education is still in its emerging stage, but it shows promising potential. For instance, imagine an AR application that visually represents the blockchain process right on your table. You could watch a virtual block being added to the chain every time a transaction is verified, with each block displaying real-time data. This kind of immersive experience could significantly enhance your understanding of how blockchains operate. Another application could be in the realm of crypto trading, where AR tools project market data into your physical space, allowing you to interact with live charts or manipulate data points in a three-dimensional space. Such tools not only make learning about cryptocurrencies more interactive but also more engaging, helping to retain complex information more effectively.

For educators and developers looking to create AR learning modules tailored to cryptocurrency education, the focus should be on interactivity and user engagement. The development process involves several stages, starting with the identification of key learning objectives. For example, if the goal is to explain how smart contracts work, the AR experience might involve a step-by-step simulation of creating and executing a smart contract. Developers must then design intuitive user interfaces that allow learners to interact with the information seamlessly. This might include touch gestures for mobile AR applications or voice commands for more immersive AR headsets. Moreover, integrating gamification elements such as scores, challenges, or unlockable content can further enhance engagement and motivation.

The future of AR in financial education, particularly in teaching about cryptocurrencies, looks incredibly promising. As AR technology continues to advance, its integration into educational tools is likely to become more sophisticated, offering more immersive and interactive learning experiences. This could revolutionize how complex financial concepts are taught, making them more understandable and accessible to a broader audience. Moreover, as cryptocurrencies and blockchain technology play a more prominent role in the global financial system, the demand for innovative educational approaches that can cater to all levels of expertise and backgrounds is expected to grow. AR could play a crucial role in meeting this educational demand, providing a bridge between complex technical knowledge and everyday understanding.

Incorporating AR into cryptocurrency education not only aids in comprehension but also prepares you for a future where technology blends more seamlessly with finance. As you continue to explore the multifaceted world of cryptocurrencies, the use of augmented reality in learning can be a powerful tool for demystifying complex concepts and enhancing your overall understanding. This engaging approach to learning not only makes education more effective but also more enjoyable, potentially attracting more individuals to the field of cryptocurrencies and fostering a more informed and savvy community of users and investors.

In wrapping up this exploration of augmented reality in cryptocurrency education, we've seen how AR can transform traditional learning methods by making complex concepts more tangible and engaging. This chapter has highlighted the potential of AR to not only enhance understanding but also to make learning about cryptocurrencies accessible to a broader audience. As we move forward, the intersection of AR technology with crypto education promises to be an exciting area of growth, offering new ways to learn, interact, and engage with the digital economy. As we continue to navigate the evolving landscape of cryptocurrencies, embracing innovative technologies like AR will be the key to staying informed and ahead in the game.

Moving into the next chapter, we'll delve into the practical aspects of applying the knowledge you've gained about cryptocurrencies, focusing on strategies for effective investment and portfolio management. This next step will equip you with the tools to not only understand but also actively participate in the cryptocurrency market, applying your learning to make informed investment decisions.

Conclusion

What a journey we've been on together! From the early pages, where we unpacked the basics of cryptocurrency and blockchain technology, to diving deep into advanced investment strategies and market analysis techniques, our exploration has been both broad and intensive. We started with fundamental concepts, understanding how digital currencies operate on decentralized platforms, and gradually advanced to mastering the tools and tactics that seasoned investors use to navigate the complex crypto markets.

Throughout this book, my aim has been to empower you with knowledge—knowledge that not only enhances your understanding but also equips you with the necessary tools to navigate the cryptocurrency space with confidence. By now, you should feel more prepared to make informed investment decisions and tackle the challenges that come with this dynamic market.

However, as we've discussed, the world of cryptocurrency never stands still. The rapid pace of innovation and the continuous evolution of technology mean that learning is an ongoing process. Staying updated with the latest developments and adapting to new technologies and regulations is crucial. It's a world that rewards the curious and the diligent—those who are willing to keep learning and evolving alongside the market itself.

The potential of cryptocurrencies extends far beyond their use as investment vehicles.

Throughout our chapters, we've seen how these digital assets are making significant impacts across various sectors, including finance and healthcare, and even by addressing societal challenges. This transformative power underscores the importance of understanding and engaging with cryptocurrencies not just for personal gain but also for their broader implications.

Yet, with great potential comes great responsibility. The volatility, the ever-changing regulatory landscapes, cybersecurity threats, and environmental concerns are real challenges that require us to approach cryptocurrency investment with care and responsibility. It's crucial to practice due diligence, employ robust risk management strategies, and make ethical investment choices that consider the long-term impacts on our community and planet.

I encourage you not just to invest but to become an active participant in cryptocurrency communities. Share your knowledge, learn from others, and contribute to a collective understanding and responsible growth of this exciting field. Engage in forums, attend meetups, and stay connected with the pulse of the crypto world.

As we look to the future, let your curiosity about emerging trends such as Decentralized Finance (DeFi), Non-Fungible Tokens (NFTs), and beyond guide you to new opportunities and innovations. The horizon is continually expanding, and the possibilities are as limitless as your willingness to explore them.

I sincerely hope this book has provided you with a solid foundation and that it serves as a springboard for your continued success in cryptocurrency investing.

Thank you for trusting me to be your guide on this incredible adventure. Here's to taking bold steps, making informed decisions, and building wealth in the ever-evolving world of cryptocurrencies. Stay curious, stay cautious, and above all, stay engaged. Happy investing!

References

- *Bitcoin, Blockchain and the History of Money* https://www.imf.org/en/Publications/fandd/issues/2018/06/bitcoin-blockchain-history-of-money-james

- *What is Blockchain Technology? How Does Blockchain Work ...* https://www.simplilearn.com/tutorials/blockchain-tutorial/blockchain-technology#:~:text=Blockchain%20is%20a%20method%20of,computers%20participating%20in%20the%20blockchain.

- *Cryptocurrency vs. Traditional Banking: Understanding the ...* https://www.globaltrademag.com/cryptocurrency-vs-traditional-banking-understanding-the-differences-and-benefits/

- *Cryptocurrency Regulations Around the World* https://www.investopedia.com/cryptocurrency-regulations-around-the-world-5202122

- *What Is a Crypto Wallet and How to Choose the Right One?* https://academy.binance.com/en/articles/crypto-wallet-types-explained

- *undefined* undefined

- *What To Know About Cryptocurrency and Scams* https://consumer.ftc.gov/articles/what-know-about-cryptocurrency-and-scams

- *7 Best Cryptocurrency Investing Strategies* https://money.usnews.com/investing/articles/best-cryptocurrency-investing-strategies

- *The 8 best indicators for crypto trading in 2024* https://www.okx.com/learn/best-crypto-indicators-trading

- *How To Read Crypto Candlestick Charts* https://www.ledger.com/academy/crypto-candlestick-charts-explained

- *undefined* undefined

- *How to Create a Well-Balanced Crypto Portfolio* https://www.fool.com/investing/stock-market/market-sectors/financials/cryptocurrency-stocks/crypto-portfolio/

- *Crypto Users Lost $2B to Hacks, Scams and Exploits in ...* https://www.coindesk.com/tech/2023/12/27/crypto-users-lost-2b-to-hacks-scams-and-exploits-in-2023-defi-says/

- *Crypto Regulations in the US—A Complete Guide (2023)* https://sumsub.com/blog/crypto-regulations-in-the-us-a-complete-guide-2023/

- *What To Know About Cryptocurrency and Scams* https://consumer.ftc.gov/articles/what-know-about-cryptocurrency-and-scams

- *5 Ways to Manage Risk When Trading Cryptocurrency* https://www.coindesk.com/learn/how-to-manage-risk-when-trading-cryptocurrency/

- *undefined* undefined

- *What Is DeFi? Understanding Decentralized Finance* https://www.forbes.com/advisor/investing/cryptocurrency/defi-decentralized-finance/

- *Crypto Staking Explained: How It Works, Types, & Risks* https://www.britannica.com/money/what-is-crypto-staking

- *How to Participate in ICOs and Token Sales - Cryptomus* https://cryptomus.com/blog/how-to-participate-in-icos-and-token-sales-a-comprehensive-guide

- *Crypto Technical Analysis: Techniques, Indicators, and ...* https://onetrading.com/blogs/crypto-technical-analysis-techniques-indicators-and-applications

- *Valuation of Cryptoassets: A Guide for Investment ...* https://rpc.cfainstitute.org/en/research/reports/2023/valuation-cryptoassets

- *Do investor sentiments drive cryptocurrency prices?* https://www.sciencedirect.com/science/article/abs/pii/S0165176521002573

- *The Impact of Global Economic Indicators on Crypto Prices* https://medium.com/@maulanaazizi/the-impact-of-global-economic-indicators-on-crypto-prices-an-in-depth-analysis-a4d26c48c0d6

- *Top 5 Real-World Use Cases of Blockchain in Healthcare Organizations* https://www.linkedin.com/pulse/top-5-real-world-use-cases-blockchain-healthcare-organizations

- *Best Smart Contract Use Cases Across Industries in 2024* https://pixelplex.io/blog/smart-contract-use-cases/

- *Crypto Remittances: How Cryptocurrency Is Transforming ...* https://blog.bake.io/crypto-remittances/

- *9 Nonprofits Harnessing Blockchain For Social Impact* https://thegivingblock.com/resources/nonprofits-using-blockchain-social-impact/

- *Debunking the narratives about cryptocurrency and financial inclusion* https://www.brookings.edu/articles/debunking-the-narratives-about-cryptocurrency-and-financial-inclusion/

- *The environmental impact of bitcoin mining explained* https://www.techtarget.com/sustainability/feature/The-environmental-impact-of-bitcoin-mining-explained

- *What to Know About Cryptocurrency and Cybersecurity Risks* https://www.cnb.com/personal-banking/insights/cryptocurrency-cybersecurity-risks.html

- *Central bank digital currency evolution in 2023 - Atlantic Council* https://www.atlanticcouncil.org/blogs/econographics/central-bank-digital-currency-evolution-in-2023-from-investigation-to-preparation/

- *Digital Assets | Internal Revenue Service* https://www.irs.gov/businesses/small-businesses-self-employed/digital-assets

- *GLOBAL CRYPTOASSET REGULATORY LANDSCAPE STUDY* https://www.jbs.cam.ac.uk/wp-content/uploads/2020/08/2019-04-ccaf-global-cryptoasset-regulatory-landscape-study.pdf

- *Best Crypto Tax Software Of May 2024* https://www.forbes.com/advisor/taxes/best-crypto-tax-software/

- *Estate Planning and Cryptocurrency* https://freemanlaw.com/estate-planning-and-cryptocurrency/

- *The 12 Best Crypto News Websites in 2024* https://coinledger.io/tools/best-crypto-news-sites

- *What To Know About Cryptocurrency and Scams* https://consumer.ftc.gov/articles/what-know-about-cryptocurrency-and-scams

- *List of the Top 30 Crypto & Blockchain Conferences in 2024* https://ninjapromo.io/best-crypto-conferences

- *Quantum Computing Could Threaten Blockchain, Crypto* https://news.bloomberglaw.com/us-law-week/quantum-computing-could-threaten-blockchain-crypto

BITCOIN INVESTING FOR BEGINNERS

Unlocking Financial Freedom with Digital Gold and Cryptocurrency

Introduction

In the early days, when Bitcoin was just another tech buzzword, I was having a casual dinner with a friend who couldn't stop talking about digital currencies. I remember nodding politely, all the while thinking, "This will never catch on." Fast forward, and not only has Bitcoin caught on, but it has exploded into a phenomenon that reshaped my view of financial investments and the very perception of money. This transformation from skeptic to advocate wasn't overnight, but it was profound—and opened my eyes to the untapped opportunities in the digital currency space.

This book is crafted around the central thesis that Bitcoin is far more than a speculative bubble; it's a revolutionary technology that offers not only substantial financial opportunities but also a chance to rethink our relationship with money. In this book you will discover Bitcoin not only as an asset but also as an innovation that may well define the future of finance.

The purpose of "Bitcoin for Beginners: How to Invest and Profit from Cryptocurrency" is simple: to break down the complexities of cryptocurrency investing, focusing particularly on Bitcoin. It's tailored for you—adults who may have heard about Bitcoin on the news or from a friend but don't have a background in technology or finance—and are looking for a clear, reliable guide to understanding and investing in Bitcoin.

What sets this book apart is its commitment to clarity and practicality. Drawing from my own journey into the world of Bitcoin, I strive to present information that is not only informative but also actionable. You won't get lost in technical jargon here. Instead, you'll find straightforward explanations accompanied by real-world advice that you can apply to your own investment decisions.

The structure of the book is designed to guide you step by step. We'll start with the origins and basics of Bitcoin, delve into different investment strategies, explore how to manage risks, and finally, look towards the future of Bitcoin. Each section builds upon the last, ensuring that when you finish the book, you'll have a comprehensive understanding of the subject.

I encourage you to not just read this book but to actively engage with it. Reflect on the discussion questions, try out the exercises, and apply what you learn to your personal financial situation. This is not just about investing in Bitcoin—it's about empowering yourself with knowledge to make informed financial decisions.

As we embark on this journey together, remember that understanding and investing in Bitcoin could be one of the most empowering financial decisions you make. My passion for financial education is the core of this book, and I am here to guide you through each step of your Bitcoin investment journey.

Let's decode the world of cryptocurrency and unlock new opportunities for growth and independence together. Welcome to "Bitcoin for Beginners."

Chapter 1

Understanding Bitcoin and Cryptocurrency

Have you ever stopped to wonder what really lies behind the hype about Bitcoin? You might have caught fragments of it on the news—jaw-dropping stories of early investors turning into overnight millionaires or ominous predictions about a digital bubble set to burst. But beyond these headlines, there's a transformative financial landscape that's been slowly redefining the very essence of money and transactions. In this chapter, we'll peel back the layers of what might just be the most significant financial revolution of our time, and no, it's not just about making a quick buck. It's about understanding a new way of thinking about currency, investment, and our economic autonomy.

What is Bitcoin? The Genesis of Digital Currency

Definition and Origin

In 2009, amidst the ashes of the most severe fiscal disasters since the Great Depression, an entity—or possibly a group—under the pseudonym Satoshi Nakamoto introduced Bitcoin to the world. This wasn't just another digital currency; it was the first decentralized digital currency. Fundamentally, Bitcoin was envisioned as an electronic cash system that was completely peer-to-peer, which meant it could simplify transactions between individuals without the need for a central authority, such as a bank or government. This radical approach to money was a direct response to the distrust in traditional financial institutions at the time, with many feeling that these entities had played fast and loose with their responsibilities and the public's trust.

Key Characteristics

Bitcoin introduces several radical features that set it apart from traditional currencies. First, it's decentralized, which means it's not controlled by any single entity. The consequences of this are enormous, as it places the power of managing currency back into the hands of the people. Secondly, Bitcoin has a limited supply— there will only ever be 21 million Bitcoins in existence. This scarcity is similar to precious metals such as gold, which have historically been used as a hedge against inflation and the devaluation of currency. Additionally, Bitcoin is divisible, meaning you can own and transact fractions of a Bitcoin (up to eight decimal places), making it accessible for small and large transactions alike. Lastly, it's portable, as Bitcoin can be sent anywhere in the world via an internet connection without the need for intermediaries and is often cheaper and faster than traditional international wire transfers.

Bitcoin's Intent

The original intent of Bitcoin was to provide an alternative to the fiat currency system by creating a method of exchange that was secure, transparent, and efficient. Distinct from traditional currencies, which can be manipulated and are often devalued by governments and financial institutions, Bitcoin operates on a model of mathematical certainty. It's built on a technology called blockchain, which ensures that every transaction is recorded in a public ledger and visible to all but is tamper-proof and secure. This system not only reduces the possibility of fraud but also eliminates the need for costly intermediaries, thereby democratizing financial transactions and giving control back to the individual user.

Cultural Impact

Bitcoin's emergence has sparked a global conversation about the future of money. It has challenged the monopoly of national currencies and central banks and has inspired a wave of technological innovation in finance that continues to this day. Other cryptocurrencies have since emerged, each offering unique solutions to different challenges, but all building on the foundational principles introduced by Bitcoin. Moreover, Bitcoin has influenced discussions on financial privacy, sovereignty, and inclusion, pushing these vital issues to the forefront of global economic conversations.

Reflection Section

To better grasp the revolutionary impact of Bitcoin, reflect on the following questions:

- How do you currently perceive the reliability and stability of traditional banks and financial institutions?

- In what ways can a decentralized currency like Bitcoin change your personal financial autonomy?

- What are the potential benefits and challenges of a currency that has a limited, predetermined supply?

Through these reflections, you can begin to understand not only the functions of Bitcoin but also its profound implications on a personal and global scale. Remember them as we continue, keep these thoughts in mind, and consider how the shift towards digital currencies might influence not just your wallet but also the broader economic landscape.

Decoding Cryptocurrency: From Blockchain to Bitcoin

Imagine walking into a room where a group of people, each holding a notebook, records every transaction you make. Each note is cross-checked for accuracy, and no single person controls the record. Instead, everyone in the room has a copy of the same book. This is a simplified glimpse into how blockchain technology, the bedrock of cryptocurrencies like Bitcoin, functions. The blockchain is fundamentally a digital ledger that is maintained by a network of multiple nodes (computers), which makes it decentralized. Every 'block' in the chain is comprised of several transactions, and each time a new one occurs, a record of the transaction is added to each participant's ledger. It's this infrastructure that underpins Bitcoin and allows it to operate securely and transparently without the need for a central authority.

Now, let's delve deeper into how blockchain powers Bitcoin. You can think of blockchain as the foundation upon which Bitcoin is built. If you want to send Bitcoin to another person, the transaction details are broadcast to a network of nodes, the computers participating in the Bitcoin network. These nodes take the information and validate the transaction using a set of cryptographic rules. This process involves miners, who compete to solve complex mathematical problems that validate the transactions; the first miner to unravel the problem will add a new block to the blockchain. This is known as the consensus mechanism, and it's crucial because it ensures that each transaction is confirmed by multiple nodes independently, securing the network from tampering and fraud.

The beauty of blockchain doesn't end with Bitcoin. Its potential applications stretch far beyond cryptocurrency. For instance, consider smart contracts, self-executing contracts with the terms directly written into code, or supply chain management, where blockchain can offer a transparent and unalterable record of product journeys from manufacturer to consumer. These applications underscore blockchain's versatility and capacity to impart efficiency and security in various domains, demonstrating its utility in automating and securing complex processes without the need for a central authority.

Blockchain's technological significance in the realm of cryptocurrency cannot be overstated. It's revolutionary because it eliminates the need for trust in financial transactions. In traditional finance, a transaction will rely heavily on third parties like credit card companies or banks to verify the exchange of money. Blockchain technology disrupts this model by allowing people to make direct transactions with confidence, knowing that the record of their exchange is secure and unchangeable. This aspect is particularly transformative in environments where the reliability of financial institutions might be questionable or where they are non-existent. By democratizing access to secure financial transactions, blockchain is not just a technical innovation; it's a facilitator of financial inclusion and autonomy.

How Bitcoin Works: The Science of Cryptocurrencies

Let's peel back the curtain on how Bitcoin actually functions under the hood. Envisage yourself wanting to send Bitcoin to a friend as a gift. You initiate the transaction by entering the amount of Bitcoin you want to send and your friend's digital wallet address. This is where things get interesting. Every Bitcoin wallet comes with two keys: a public key, which you can think of as a mailbox, and a private key, which acts much like a key to that mailbox. Your friend's public key is used to deposit the Bitcoins, but it's the private key that's crucial because it allows them to access and use the Bitcoins you send. This pair of keys ensures that the transaction is secure. Only the person with the correct private key can access the Bitcoins sent to a specific public key, safeguarding against unauthorized access.

Once you've initiated the transaction, it doesn't just float straight over to your friend. It first needs to be verified and recorded on the blockchain. This is where miners come into play, as they use powerful computers to resolve intricate mathematical problems that validate your transaction. This process is known as proof-of-work. It serves a dual purpose: securing the network from fraudulent transactions and creating new Bitcoins. When a miner successfully solves the mathematical puzzle, this adds a 'block' of transactions to the blockchain. This is no small feat; hence, the network rewards miners by giving them new Bitcoins. This reward halves approximately every four years and is known as the 'halving,' which is why Bitcoin is often compared to precious metals, such as gold—it gets harder and more resource-intensive to mine over time.

Security in Bitcoin goes beyond just the transaction mechanism. Cryptographic techniques are the bedrock of its security features. Bitcoin uses a specific type of cryptography known as the SHA-256 hash function, which turns transaction information into a series of numbers and letters that is virtually impossible to predict. This protects the integrity of your transaction by making it almost impossible for anyone to alter the transaction data. Each block on the blockchain comprises its unique hash and also that of the previous block, creating a link between them. This chain of hashes is what makes the blockchain secure and Immutable. If someone attempts to alter a transaction, it changes the hash of the block. Since the blocks are linked, altering one hash would require altering all subsequent hashes, which is computationally impractical.

Now, consider the decentralized nature of Bitcoin's network. Instead of having a central point of control, Bitcoin's ledger is distributed across a network of nodes, each having a replica of the complete blockchain and working to maintain its integrity and accuracy. When a new block is added to the blockchain, each node independently verifies it against the existing blockchain. If a majority of nodes agree that the new block is valid, it is accepted into the blockchain. This decentralization not only enhances security but also increases transparency and makes Bitcoin resistant to censorship. If there's ever a disagreement about a transaction (known as a fork), the blockchain can split into two paths. One path follows the new, contested rules, while the other continues under the old rules, allowing the community to decide which blockchain to continue to use based on consensus, ensuring that the network remains democratic and resilient.

Understanding these processes illuminates why Bitcoin is often hailed as a revolutionary financial technology. It's not merely about the potential monetary gains; it's about the empowerment that comes from having a secure, efficient, and transparent way to transact without the need for old-style financial intermediaries. This technology could potentially reshape the global economic landscape, making transactions quicker, cheaper, and more accessible to people around the world who are currently outside the reach of traditional banking services. As we continue to explore the implications and applications of Bitcoin, it becomes clear that its true power lies not just in its ability to generate wealth but in its potential to change how we think about and engage with the financial systems of the world.

Comparing Bitcoin and Traditional Banking

When you think about traditional banking, images of massive buildings, long lines, and heaps of paperwork might come to mind. Now, imagine an alternative where transactions are as easy as sending an email without the need for a brick-and-mortar institution acting as the middleman. This is where Bitcoin steps into the picture, challenging centuries-old banking practices with its unique approach to managing transactions. The differences between Bitcoin and traditional banking are stark, primarily revolving around the concepts of privacy, transaction speed, international transfers, and user autonomy.

Privacy in traditional banking is a complex issue; banks are required to collect personal information, ostensibly to protect against fraud, but also make your financial activity an open book to various agencies by default. Bitcoin offers a different approach. Transactions are recorded on a public ledger, yes, but the identities of the parties involved are represented only by their wallet addresses—random strings of numbers and letters. This pseudonymity allows users a degree of privacy that's hard to find in standard financial systems.

Moreover, the speed of transactions with Bitcoin contrasts sharply with traditional banking, where transfers can take days to clear, especially if crossing national borders. Bitcoin transactions can be confirmed in as rapidly as ten minutes and, once added to the blockchain, are considered secure and irreversible.

International transfers with Bitcoin also offer a distinct advantage over traditional methods, which can be costly and laden with red tape. Bitcoin simplifies the process, allowing direct transfers without the need for currency exchange or third-party intervention. This not only cuts down on fees but also on the time it takes to send money across borders. It's no wonder that people from countries with unstable currencies or restrictive financial systems find Bitcoin particularly appealing. Lastly, Bitcoin places a great degree of autonomy in the hands of its users. Without the need for a central authority, individuals have complete control over their own digital assets. This means no arbitrary limits on transactions, no exorbitant fees for certain types of transfers, and no risk of asset seizure by corrupt or financially unstable governments.

However, as much as Bitcoin presents advantages over conventional systems, it's not without its challenges. Scalability remains a significant issue. Bitcoin's network currently handles only a fraction of the transactions per second as compared to traditional credit card networks. Efforts to improve this through various means, including the Lightning Network and Segregated Witness (SegWit), are ongoing, but the problem is far from solved. Volatility is another challenge. The cost of Bitcoin can swing wildly within a short period, influenced by factors like regulatory news, market sentiment, and technological developments. This volatility can be a barrier for its adoption as a daily currency rather than just an asset for speculation.

Furthermore, regulatory acceptance varies widely from one jurisdiction to another, affecting everything from Bitcoin's legality to how it's taxed. Countries like Japan have embraced cryptocurrency, providing clear regulatory frameworks that help integrate it into daily financial activities. Others remain skeptical, imposing strict regulations or outright bans that complicate Bitcoin's adoption and use. These challenges highlight the complex landscape that Bitcoin must navigate to gain broader acceptance and fulfill its potential as a valid alternative to traditional financial systems.

Looking ahead, the potential for Bitcoin to either complement or disrupt traditional banking remains a topic of much debate. On the one hand, its advantages in terms of transaction speed, cost, and user autonomy present a compelling case for its integration into the existing financial ecosystem. Banks are already exploring ways to harness blockchain technology for faster and more secure transactions. On the other hand, Bitcoin's decentralization and ability to operate outside the traditional finance system pose a disruptive threat to established banking institutions, potentially diminishing their role in the global economy.

As we continue to explore the intricacies of Bitcoin and its place in the financial world, it's clear that its journey is still in its early stages. The coming years will undoubtedly bring further challenges, opportunities, and innovations that will inevitably shape the future of both Bitcoin and traditional banking. How these two systems will interact, compete, or integrate is still unfolding, and the implications for investors, consumers, and financial professionals are vast and varied. As with any emerging technology, the landscape is dynamic, and the potential for transformation is enormous.

Key Bitcoin Terminologies Explained

Navigating the world of Bitcoin can sometimes feel like learning a new language. From 'Satoshi' to 'wallets,' understanding these terms is critical for anyone looking to participate in Bitcoin, whether it's for investing purposes or simply to better understand this digital currency revolution. Let's break down some of these essential terms in a way that's easy to grasp.

The lowest Bitcoin unit is called a 'Satoshi' after its mysterious creator, Satoshi Nakamoto. One Satoshi is to Bitcoin what a penny is to a dollar—only much, much smaller. To put it in perspective, one Bitcoin is equivalent to 100,000,000 Satoshis. This divisibility is part of what makes Bitcoin suitable for micro-transactions, unlike traditional currencies, which are often limited by physical coins or small denomination bills.

When we talk about a 'wallet' in Bitcoin terms, we're not referring to a physical wallet you carry in your pocket, but rather a digital one. This wallet is where you store your Bitcoin. There are two main types of wallets: digital wallets, which are software programs that can store your Bitcoin online, on your computer or mobile device, and hardware wallets, which are physical devices that keep your Bitcoin stored offline. Hardware wallets are often considered more secure because they aren't connected to the internet, which shields them from hacking attempts and other online vulnerabilities.

Understanding 'hash rate' is critical to grasping how Bitcoin mining works. The hash rate measures the performance of the miners—the individuals and companies who contribute the computing power necessary to maintain the Bitcoin network and process transactions.

In more technical terms, the hash rate is the speed at which a miner's hardware operates as it tries to solve the cryptographic puzzles that add new blocks to the blockchain. A higher hash rate increases a miner's chance of finding the next block and receiving the Bitcoin reward. This rate not only reflects the health and security of the Bitcoin network but also affects how quickly transactions are processed.

'Nodes' are the individual computers that connect to the Bitcoin network, each hosting a copy of the entire blockchain. These nodes play a crucial role in the consensus process, working to verify the legitimacy of transactions and blocks. They're the backbone that keeps the Bitcoin network decentralized and secure. Each node independently checks transactions against the existing blockchain, rejecting those that don't conform to the network rules. This decentralized verification process is fundamental to Bitcoin's security and trustworthiness.

A 'fork' in the Bitcoin world occurs when there is a change to the blockchain software that creates two different versions of the history. This usually happens when the community behind Bitcoin is divided about the best way to move forward. Forks can be planned as part of the network's upgrade process, or they can be contentious, leading to a permanent split and creating a new cryptocurrency.

Let's now discuss 'public and private keys.' These are part of the cryptography that Bitcoin uses to secure transactions. Each Bitcoin wallet may contain several private keys, which are saved in the wallet file and are mathematically connected to all Bitcoin addresses created for the wallet. Essentially, your private key is your digital identity for Bitcoin transactions. It's what you use to sign transactions to prove you own the Bitcoins associated with your address, and you must keep it secure. If someone obtains access to your private keys, they can spend your Bitcoin. On the other hand, the public key is derived from the private well and can be shared with anyone. It's like your bank account number that you'd give to someone who needs to send you money.

Lastly, we have 'altcoins' and 'ICOs ' Altcoins, or alternative coins, are cryptocurrencies other than Bitcoin. Many altcoins are built on the basic framework provided by Bitcoin but aim to improve or offer different capabilities. Examples include Ethereum, Ripple, and Litecoin, each with its own unique features and uses. Initial Coin Offerings, or ICOs, are a fundraising mechanism used mainly by startup companies offering products and services related to cryptocurrency and blockchain space. ICOs can be a risky investment because they're relatively unregulated, but they can also provide the potential for significant returns, similar to early investments in startups.

Understanding these terms not only enriches your knowledge of how Bitcoin operates but also enhances your ability to participate in conversations about cryptocurrency. Whether you're discussing investment opportunities, exploring the technology, or simply satisfying your curiosity, a solid grasp of these concepts is invaluable. As you continue to explore Bitcoin and perhaps even start to interact with the system, keep these definitions in mind. They'll serve as your guideposts in the dynamic and ever-evolving landscape of cryptocurrency.

Chapter 2

The Historical Context and Economic Impact

Have you ever wondered how money evolved from simple barter systems to the complex digital currencies we use today? It's a fascinating journey that not only reflects technological advancements but also shifts in societal needs and values. In this chapter, we'll explore the tapestry of monetary evolution and carve out a space for Bitcoin in the grand scheme of things. This exploration isn't just academic; understanding where Bitcoin fits into the history of money can give us insight into its potential future and the role it might play in reshaping our global financial landscape.

A Brief History of Money and Where Bitcoin Fits

From Barter to Digital: Tracing the Evolution of Money

The story of money is as old as civilization itself. In the beginning, there was barter—simple, straightforward trade. I give you something you need, and in return, you give me something I need. However, as communities expanded and trade grew more complex, carrying around the items you wanted to trade became impractical. Enter commodity money—goods that held universal value, like salt or gold, used to represent wealth. These were portable, durable, and, importantly, divisible, making trade easier and more efficient.

Fast forward a few centuries, and we see the introduction of metal coins and, eventually, paper money—each innovation driven by the need for more convenient, scalable methods of trade. Paper money, a representation of value stored somewhere else, marked a significant shift. It was a promise, a bearer of trust that the paper could be exchanged for something of equal value. As societies continued to evolve, so too did their financial needs, which led to the creation of credit cards and electronic banking. These digital transactions enabled commerce on a scale previously unimaginable, connecting global economies in real time.

The Emergence of Digital Currency

As the internet began to dominate the landscape of communication and commerce, it was only a matter of time before digital currencies emerged. These were currencies born of the digital age, meant to simplify transactions in an increasingly online world. Initially, digital currencies were centralized and created by companies as tokens for use within specific online communities. However, they were limited by the trust placed in these central authorities—trust that was not always upheld.

Bitcoin, introduced in 2009, revolutionized this concept by creating a decentralized digital currency. For the first time, digital money could be sent directly from one person to another without going through a bank or payment gateway. This was made possible by blockchain technology—a decentralized record that chronicles all transactions across a network of computers. The implications were profound, as this not only minimized the risk of fraud but also democratized financial transactions, removing the control from central institutions and placing it back into the hands of individuals.

Bitcoin's Unique Place in Monetary History

Bitcoin stands out in the history of money for its ability to solve the double-spend problem without the need for a trusted authority. In traditional digital transactions, a central authority had to verify that each unit of currency hadn't been spent twice. With Bitcoin, this verification is decentralized, spread across a network of nodes that see and verify each transaction. This not only enhances security but also aligns with a growing desire for transparency and autonomy in financial dealings.

Implications for the Future of Money

As we look to the future, Bitcoin's potential to influence the global financial system continues to grow. It challenges traditional banking infrastructures, offers new forms of financial inclusivity, and may even redefine what we consider as 'money.' Could Bitcoin or other cryptocurrencies replace traditional money? It's a possibility worth considering. More likely, however, is a future in which digital and traditional forms of money coexist, each serving unique needs within the global economy. This coexistence could lead to a more diversified, resilient, and democratic financial system globally.

In navigating this evolution, remember that the steps we take now—how we regulate, adopt, and integrate technologies like Bitcoin—will shape the financial landscapes of tomorrow. As you reflect on Bitcoin's place in the tapestry of monetary history, consider how its principles of decentralization and transparency could influence not only financial systems but also broader societal structures. Imagine a world where financial inclusivity is the norm and the barriers to economic participation are dramatically reduced. This isn't just theoretical; it's a potential future that grows more tangible with each transaction recorded on the blockchain.

As we continue to explore Bitcoin's role and influence, keep in mind the broader implications of this digital revolution. The shift toward decentralized currencies could herald a new era of economic interaction, one in which power is distributed more evenly and the rules of engagement are rewritten for the betterment of all.

Bitcoin and the Concept of Decentralization

Decentralization is a term that often pops up in discussions about Bitcoin, but what does it really mean, especially in the context of finance and technology? At its core, decentralization refers to the distribution of power away from a central authority. In financial systems, this means moving control from traditional institutions like banks and governments to a distributed network, typically using technology. Bitcoin embodies this concept through its blockchain technology, where every transaction is verified by multiple nodes (computers) across the globe rather than by a single central entity. This significant attribute of Bitcoin is not just a technical detail; it's the philosophical backbone that makes Bitcoin uniquely positioned to redefine aspects of our financial systems.

The contrast between decentralized systems like Bitcoin and centralized financial systems is stark. Centralized systems operate through central authorities such as banks, which control transaction verifications, the creation of new units of currency, and the overarching rules of their operation. These systems have been the foundation of our economies for centuries; however, they come with drawbacks. Centralization can lead to inefficiencies, such as slow transaction times and higher costs due to intermediaries. Moreover, they can be prone to corruption and mismanagement—risks that are borne by the users. On the other hand, decentralized systems like Bitcoin allow transactions to be verified by a consensus among participants, dramatically reducing the need for intermediaries. This can lead to speedier transaction times and lower costs. Additionally, the decentralized nature of Bitcoin minimizes the risks of corruption and central points of failure.

However, while decentralization has its advantages, it also impacts financial autonomy in profound ways. By reducing reliance on traditional financial institutions, Bitcoin allows individuals to have more control over their financial transactions. You're no longer bound by the fees, terms, and conditions imposed by banks. More importantly, this shift can empower individuals in underbanked or unstable regions to access financial services without the need for a physical bank. This aspect of Bitcoin is transformative, offering a level of financial autonomy that was previously unattainable for many.

Despite these benefits, decentralization comes with its own set of challenges. Regulatory issues are a significant hurdle. Without central oversight, it can be difficult for governments to enforce financial regulations such as anti-money laundering (AML) and know-your-customer (KYC) standards. This can make Bitcoin a potential tool for illegal activities. Furthermore, the decentralized nature of Bitcoin could lead to fragmentation in financial policies if not integrated thoughtfully within existing monetary systems. Addressing these challenges requires innovative regulatory approaches that balance the need for control with the benefits of decentralization. Regulators might need to develop new frameworks that recognize the unique attributes of decentralized systems without stifling their growth.

Another challenge is the potential for misuse. Without centralized control, bad actors could potentially manipulate transaction verifications or take advantage of the anonymity provided by cryptocurrencies like Bitcoin for nefarious purposes. However, the community-driven nature of Bitcoin has led to the development of various protocols that enhance security and transparency. For instance, continuous updates to the Bitcoin network protocol aim to address vulnerabilities as they arise. Moreover, the transparency of the blockchain allows transactions to be publicly tracked, adding a layer of accountability that is often absent in traditional systems.

In navigating these challenges, the role of community consensus in the development and governance of Bitcoin becomes crucial. Unlike centralized systems, where decisions are made by a few, decisions in Bitcoin's network are made by consensus, offering a democratic approach to financial governance. This not only helps mitigate risks but also ensures that changes to the network reflect the collective interest of its users.

As we explore the broader implications of Bitcoin's decentralization, it's clear that this concept is reshaping not just the technical landscape of transactions but also the very notion of financial autonomy and security. Decentralization challenges the traditional paradigms of financial governance and opens up new possibilities for user empowerment and systemic resilience. While the road ahead is fraught with challenges, the potential for positive change makes it an exciting area of development in the evolution of money.

How Bitcoin Challenges the Fiat Currency System

When you hold a dollar, euro, or any other fiat currency, you're essentially holding a piece of a country's economic system. The value of this currency hinges mainly on the government's ability to maintain it; however, this system isn't without its flaws. Fiat money, which is money without intrinsic value that a government has declared to be legal tender, is vulnerable to inflation. This often occurs when governments print more money to cover their debts, effectively diluting the value of existing money. Moreover, fiat currencies are inextricably linked to the political and economic stability of the governments that issue them. In times of political unrest or poor economic management, the value of fiat money can fluctuate wildly.

In stark contrast, Bitcoin stands as a currency untethered from governmental oversight. Its decentralized nature means no single entity can dictate its value or arbitrarily decide to increase its supply. Bitcoin's protocol caps its total supply at 21 million coins, a stark contrast to government-sanctioned currencies, which may be printed at the whim of policymakers. This integral scarceness is similar to precious metals such as gold, which have historically retained value due to their limited nature. This feature of Bitcoin is x particularly appealing to those who wish to hedge against inflation. Unlike fiat currencies, which can lose value over time, Bitcoin's design inherently avoids this downside, which makes it a deflationary asset.

The real-world implications of this are profound, especially in countries that experience hyperinflation. Consider Venezuela, where hyperinflation reached 1,000,000% in 2018, rendering the local currency, the bolivar, nearly worthless. In such economies, Bitcoin offers an attractive alternative. It provides a stable source of value and means of transaction outside the rapidly depreciating local currency. In Zimbabwe, another country plagued by severe inflation, Bitcoin has become so in demand that it has traded at rates significantly higher than in more stable economies. This high premium reflects its perceived value as a stabilizing force, where locals turn to Bitcoin to conserve their savings and engage in commerce without the constant fear of their money losing value overnight.

Moreover, Bitcoin is inherently resistant to censorship and seizure. Each transaction is recorded on a blockchain, a distributed ledger that no single party controls. This architecture not only makes Bitcoin transactions nearly impossible to censor but also protects against seizure. In regions where political unrest or economic instability is prevalent, this aspect of Bitcoin is particularly critical. For instance, during political protests in Nigeria in 2020, government authorities targeted the bank accounts of activists. In response, many turned to Bitcoin and other cryptocurrencies to fund their activities, circumventing governmental control and ensuring the continuation of their efforts. This resistance to censorship and seizure not only makes Bitcoin an attractive financial tool in such contexts but also underscores its role in promoting financial sovereignty.

In these ways, Bitcoin stands not merely as an alternative to fiat currencies but as a critique of the system itself. It challenges the conventional financial and political structures that have governed how money is created, valued, and exchanged for centuries. As Bitcoin continues to gain traction, it forces us to rethink the very fabric of economic policy and monetary control. Whether it will replace fiat currencies entirely remains to be seen, but its impact on how we think about and use money is undeniable. As we navigate this evolving landscape, Bitcoin remains a key player in the dialogue about not only our economic futures but also about the balance of power between governments and the governed.

Understanding Bitcoin's Role in Global Finance

In the realm of global finance, Bitcoin is making waves not just as a speculative asset but as a functional currency that's reshaping how we think about and engage in international transactions. The traditional banking system, with its layers of intermediaries and hefty fees, often makes moving money across borders a costly and time-consuming endeavor. Bitcoin, on the other hand, streamlines this process significantly. By utilizing blockchain technology, Bitcoin allows for transfers that bypass traditional financial intermediaries, offering a direct route from sender to receiver. This not only slashes transaction fees but also drastically reduces the time it takes for funds to be transferred across national borders. Imagine sending money from the U.S. to Australia and having it arrive in minutes rather than days and at a fraction of the cost of a wire transfer or remittance service. This efficiency makes Bitcoin an attractive option for businesses and individuals looking to operate on a global scale, ensuring faster and cheaper transactions that can keep pace with the speed of international commerce.

Moreover, Bitcoin is significantly impacting the world of remittances, where immigrants send money back to their home countries. Old-style payment channels often come with high fees, which can be burdensome for individuals sending money home regularly. Bitcoin and other cryptocurrencies offer a much cheaper alternative with fees that are typically a small fraction of what would be paid through conventional remittance services. The lower cost will make a substantial difference in the lives of families receiving these funds, ensuring that more money actually makes its way into the hands of those who need it rather than being lost to transaction fees. Furthermore, the accessibility of Bitcoin transactions via smartphones means that these transfers can be made without the need for a bank account, which is an essential benefit in regions where banking services are limited or non-existent.

The incorporation of Bitcoin into existing financial systems is also progressing, with several banks and financial institutions beginning to recognize the potential benefits of cryptocurrency. Some are exploring the use of Bitcoin for transaction services, while others are investing in cryptocurrency exchanges or creating their own digital currency platforms. This integration is a testament to Bitcoin's growing legitimacy and its potential to complement traditional financial services. By partnering with existing financial institutions, Bitcoin can leverage the strengths of both the new and old financial systems, creating a hybrid model that offers more flexibility and efficiency than could be achieved by either one alone. Such partnerships can help connect the traditional financial world and the expanding crypto economy, facilitating smoother transactions that incorporate the best aspects of both worlds.

Finally, Bitcoin holds tremendous potential for enhancing financial inclusion worldwide. Anyone can create a Bitcoin wallet using only a smartphone and internet access and start receiving and sending funds. This accessibility is particularly crucial for the unbanked populations of the world, who may lack access to traditional banking services but can still participate in the global economy through Bitcoin. The implications of this are profound, offering economic empowerment to millions who have previously been marginalized by the conventional financial system. By providing these individuals with the tools to save, invest, and transact on a global scale, Bitcoin is not just a currency or an investment; it's a tool for social change, enabling greater participation in the economic processes that shape our world.

As Bitcoin continues to evolve and become part of the global financial landscape, its role as a catalyst for economic change becomes increasingly apparent. Whether it's transforming how we think about international transactions, reducing the cost of remittances, partnering with traditional financial institutions, or promoting financial inclusion, Bitcoin is proving to be a significant force in the redefinition of global finance. As we move forward, the continued adaptation and integration of Bitcoin will likely unlock new possibilities for efficiency, inclusivity, and innovation in financial services, reshaping the economic landscape in ways that are currently hard to imagine.

The Philosophy Behind Bitcoin and Economic Freedom

The seeds of Bitcoin were sown in a soil rich with libertarian ideas, emphasizing individual liberty, skepticism of authority, and the importance of privacy. The creators and early adopters of Bitcoin were heavily influenced by these ideas, viewing the cryptocurrency as a tool to reduce or eliminate the role of government in personal transactions. This philosophical backbone sets Bitcoin apart from traditional currencies and embeds it with a potential for societal change that goes beyond mere financial transactions.

Bitcoin was born following the 2008 financial crisis—a time when trust in global financial institutions and governments was notably eroding. The creators of Bitcoin envisioned a system where monetary transactions no longer required approval from banks or governments, thus sidestepping the pitfalls of political and economic mismanagement seen in the fiat currency systems. This vision is encapsulated in Bitcoin's decentralized nature, where transactions are verified by a network of peers rather than a central authority.

This not only enhances privacy by masking the identities of the parties involved behind cryptographic keys but also aligns with the libertarian value of minimizing state control and surveillance.

Moreover, Bitcoin's potential as a tool for economic empowerment is immense. By circumventing traditional financial institutions, it offers individuals unprecedented control over their financial dealings. For someone in a developing country without access to a bank, Bitcoin can provide a gateway to participate in global transactions and access services previously out of reach. This empowerment extends to combating inflation and financial instability often seen in countries with less stable economic systems. By providing a more stable store of value than their national currencies, Bitcoin gives individuals a way to preserve their wealth independently of their government's economic decisions.

Despite its potential, Bitcoin is not without its critics. Some argue that its emphasis on anonymity makes it an ideal conduit for illegal activities, such as money laundering or funding terrorism. However, these concerns are often countered by the benefits Bitcoin offers in terms of financial privacy and security. While it's true that Bitcoin, like any tool, can be misused, it also provides legitimate users with protection from identity theft and financial fraud by keeping their personal information private. Furthermore, the transparency of the blockchain ledger ensures that all transactions are traceable, which can actually aid law enforcement in tracking down illicit activity more effectively than with traditional cash transactions.

Looking to the future, the widespread adoption of Bitcoin could significantly alter the landscape of global economic systems. Imagine a world where financial transactions are seamlessly conducted across borders without the need for currency exchange or third-party verification. This could lead to a more interconnected and efficient global economy, with lower transaction costs and higher accessibility. The decentralization of financial power could also lead to greater economic democratization, where individuals have a greater say in their economic destinies without undue influence from centralized authorities.

This vision of the future is not without challenges. The volatility of Bitcoin, regulatory hurdles, and the technological complexities of blockchain technology are significant barriers to its widespread adoption. However, as the technology matures and more people become aware of its benefits, these challenges may be overcome, leading to a more decentralized and equitable global financial system.

Reflecting on these points, Bitcoin offers more than just an alternative to traditional financial systems. It embodies a philosophy of economic freedom and empowerment, challenging us to rethink the role of money in society. As we continue to explore Bitcoin's capabilities and address its challenges, we may find that its most significant impact is not on our wallets but on our very concepts of freedom and autonomy in an increasingly digital world.

As we wrap up this exploration of Bitcoin's philosophical underpinnings, we see a digital currency that is much more than a technological novelty. It is a manifestation of a desire for greater financial freedom and a challenge to the traditional power structures that govern our economic lives. Moving forward, the journey of Bitcoin will undoubtedly be fascinating, filled with debates, innovations, and, perhaps, a redefinition of money itself. In the next chapter, we delve deeper into the practicalities of Bitcoin—how to acquire, store, and use it effectively—guiding you through the technical aspects of handling Bitcoin while considering its broader implications.

Chapter 3

Getting Started with Bitcoin

Imagine standing at the threshold of a new financial universe where the control of your money is entirely in your hands, free from the grip of traditional banking systems. That's the promise of Bitcoin, and it all begins with setting up your very first Bitcoin wallet. Think of this wallet not just as a tool but as your personal gateway to buying, storing, and using Bitcoin. It's where the magic happens, and today, I'll guide you through every step to create and secure your Bitcoin wallet, ensuring you start on the right foot in your Bitcoin adventure.

Setting Up Your First Bitcoin Wallet

Choosing the Right Wallet

When it comes to storing your Bitcoin, you have a few options, each with its own set of benefits and considerations. There are three main types of wallets to choose from: software wallets, hardware wallets, and paper wallets.

Software wallets are apps or programs that you can download to your computer or phone and are an easy way to access and manage your Bitcoin, making them ideal for everyday use and small amounts of money. However, they are only as secure as the device they are on, so if your device is hacked, there's a risk your Bitcoin could be stolen.

On the other hand, a hardware wallet is a physical device designed specifically for storing cryptocurrency. It looks a bit like a USB drive and is considered one of the safest options available. A hardware wallet will keep your personal keys offline and away from potential online vulnerabilities, offering an excellent balance between security and convenience for larger amounts of Bitcoin or long-term holdings.

Paper wallets are exactly what they sound like: your Bitcoin private and public keys printed out on a piece of paper. While they are completely safe from hackers, they come with their own risks. If the paper is lost, damaged, or destroyed, so are your Bitcoin. Paper wallets are best for those who want to store Bitcoin away for a long time and can ensure the safekeeping of the paper.

Choosing the right wallet depends largely on how you plan to use your Bitcoin. If you're planning on using Bitcoin for daily transactions, a software wallet might be the way to go. If you're looking at Bitcoin as a long-term investment, a hardware wallet provides the security you'll need. And for those considering Bitcoin as a legacy to hold onto for many years, a paper wallet—while requiring careful handling—could be the perfect choice.

Step-by-Step Wallet Setup

Let's walk through setting up a software wallet, as it's the most common choice for beginners. First, choose a reputable wallet provider. Look for one with a strong track record of security and user-friendly features. Once you've downloaded the app or software, the next step is creating your account. This usually involves setting a strong password and, in some cases, linking your email or mobile phone for security purposes.

Navigating the user interface is your next step. Spend some time familiarizing yourself with the layout. Look for features like the 'send' and 'receive' buttons, your transaction history, and your current balance. Most wallets will also have a section for managing your security settings—don't skip this.

Backup and Recovery

Backing up your wallet is crucial. Most wallets provide you with a recovery phrase when you set them up. This phrase should consist of 12 to 24 words and is used to restore your wallet if your computer or phone is lost or damaged. Write this phrase down on paper, then place it in a safe place where only you can access it. Never store your recovery phrase digitally or share it with anyone else.

Initial Security Measures

To protect your wallet from unauthorized access, strong passwords are a must, but don't stop there. Enable two-factor authentication (2FA) if your wallet supports it. This adds additional security by requiring not just your password but also a code sent to your phone or email when a transaction is made or if any important change is made to your account.

Other security measures include regularly updating your wallet software and keeping the devices on which your wallet is installed secure. Remember, the safety of your Bitcoin wallet is entirely in your hands, and taking these steps can help ensure the security of your digital currency.

By following these steps, you can set up and secure your first Bitcoin wallet, positioning yourself to safely participate in the exciting world of Bitcoin. Whether you're buying your first fraction of a Bitcoin or preparing to manage a more significant investment, these foundational steps are critical to your success in the cryptocurrency space.

Secure Purchasing of Bitcoin: A Step-by-Step Guide

Navigating the world of Bitcoin exchanges can feel like a maze, especially when you're trying to pinpoint the perfect one for your needs. Selecting a reputable Bitcoin exchange is your first crucial step toward buying Bitcoin securely. In this vast sea of options, focus on a few key aspects: security features, user reviews, fee structure, and regulatory compliance. A well-reputed exchange usually boasts robust security measures, such as two-factor authentication, cold storage options for customer funds, and insured custodial services. Take the time to read reviews from other users to gauge their experiences—both positive and negative—and pay attention to the fee structure, as well, since fees can vary significantly between exchanges and can affect your buying power. Lastly, ensure the exchange complies with regulations, particularly those related to anti-money laundering (AML) and know your customer (KYC) policies. Not only does this add a layer of security, but it also ensures the exchange is operating under strict guidelines that protect its users.

Once you've chosen an exchange that feels right, setting up an account is your next step. This process typically starts with registering your basic information, followed by a more detailed identity verification process. The KYC procedures are crucial as they help avert fraud and confirm that only legitimate users are trading on the platform. You'll probably need to provide a government-issued ID, proof of address, and possibly a recent photo to verify your identity. While this might seem cumbersome, it's a critical step in safeguarding your investments.

Now, let's talk about making your first Bitcoin purchase, which can be thrilling but also a bit daunting. Most exchanges offer a straightforward process to buy Bitcoin, usually starting with depositing fiat currency—such as US dollars (USD,) euros (EUR,) or British pounds sterling (GBP)—into your account. Once your funds are deposited, you're ready to buy. When placing an order, you'll find options like 'market orders' and 'limit orders.' A market order buys Bitcoin instantly at current market price, whereas a limit order lets you set a specific price at which you want to buy. The latter can be helpful if you expect the price to drop and want to lock in a lower purchase price. Understanding this often helps you make informed decisions that align with your investment strategy.

After purchasing Bitcoin, the paramount step is transferring your new digital asset to a personal wallet, reinforcing the security of your investment. While keeping Bitcoin on an exchange is convenient for trading, exchanges are more vulnerable to hacks. Transferring your Bitcoin involves locating the 'withdraw' or 'send' function on the exchange, entering your personal wallet's address, and specifying the amount of Bitcoin you wish to transfer. Double-check the address before confirming the transaction to avoid irreversible mistakes. Additionally, be mindful of transaction fees, which are required to process and confirm your transaction on the blockchain. These fees can vary based on how busy the network is at the time of your transfer, so it's wise to consider these costs when planning your purchase.

By walking through these steps carefully, you ensure that your initiation into the Bitcoin world is not only exciting but also secure. Remember, each step, from choosing an exchange to transferring funds to your wallet, builds upon the last, fortifying the security and integrity of your Bitcoin transactions. As you become more familiar with these processes, you'll find yourself navigating them with greater confidence and precision, which will pave the way for more advanced ventures in your Bitcoin journey.

Understanding and Protecting Your Private Keys

When you first dive into the world of Bitcoin, you'll often hear about the critical importance of "private keys." But what exactly are these, and why do they play such a pivotal role in the security of your Bitcoin assets? Think of private keys as the most guarded part of your Bitcoin wallet—the part that allows you to unlock and control your Bitcoin. Essentially, a private key is a sophisticated form of coding that allows a user to access their cryptocurrency. It's a unique string of characters known only to you, much like a super-secure password. Each private key is mathematically linked to a wallet address (your public key) but is not publicly disclosed. It's what keeps your Bitcoin secure and ensures that only you can access it.

The generation of these private keys is a marvel of modern cryptography. When you set up a new wallet, the software randomly generates a private key, which in turn generates a public key. The relationship between the two is irreversible—you can easily create a public key from a private key, but not the other way around. This one-way street is vital because it keeps your private key secure even though your public key is shared with the world. Understanding this mechanism is essential because the security and integrity of your Bitcoin transactions depend heavily on the confidentiality of your private key.

The risks associated with exposing your private key are severe. If someone else obtains it, they can transfer all of your Bitcoin to another account—and this action is irreversible. The most common ways private keys are exposed include phishing attacks, where scammers trick you into revealing your key; malware, which can log your keystrokes or steal wallet files; and even physical theft or loss. Each of these scenarios will leave your digital assets vulnerable, highlighting the need for stringent security measures.

To manage and store your private keys effectively, adhering to best practices Is non-negotiable. Ono of the most secure methods is using a hardware wallet. These devices store your private keys offline, isolated from online vulnerabilities such as hackers and viruses. More importantly, they allow you to make transactions online while keeping your private keys away from your computer or smartphone. Avoid storing significant amounts of Bitcoin in wallets that are continuously connected to the internet (often referred to as 'hot wallets'). Instead, consider using 'cold storage' options like paper wallets or hardware devices for large amounts or long-term holdings.

Another critical practice is never to store your private keys in plain text files or take digital photographs of paper wallets. Instead, write them down on paper and store them in a secure location, such as a safety deposit box. Multiple backups in geographically diverse locations can also safeguard against the risk of physical damage or loss.

So, what should you do if your private keys are lost or compromised? First, if you suspect that your private key has been stolen but you still have control over your wallet, transfer your funds to a new wallet immediately using a newly generated private key. If you've lost your private key, recovery can be challenging and sometimes impossible. This is why many wallets provide a mnemonic recovery phrase—a series of words generated at the setup of your wallet. This phrase, which can be used to regenerate your private key, should be written down and stored as securely as the key itself.

When dealing with private keys, the predominant theme is clear: the security of your Bitcoin hinges on the integrity and confidentiality of your private keys. By understanding their role, actively protecting them, and preparing for potential emergencies, you can ensure that your digital assets remain under your control, safeguarding your investments and giving you peace of mind in the unpredictable realm of cryptocurrency.

Common Mistakes to Avoid as a Bitcoin Beginner

Navigating the exciting yet intricate world of Bitcoin can be a rewarding experience, but this also comes with its own set of pitfalls that can trip up even the most enthusiastic beginner. Understanding some common oversights and errors can help you manage your digital assets more securely and with greater confidence. Let's explore some of these typical missteps so you can avoid them.

The importance of robust security practices cannot be overstated in the realm of cryptocurrency. A common oversight many newcomers make is the reuse of passwords on numerous platforms. This can lead to a domino effect where one compromised account can lead to breaches across all your accounts, including your Bitcoin wallet. Always use unique, strong passwords for each account, and consider using a reputable password manager to keep track of them. Additionally, while it may seem like a small step, enabling two-factor authentication (2FA) on all accounts that support it, including your Bitcoin wallet and exchange accounts, provides an extra layer of security that can thwart attempts at unauthorized access. Moreover, always ensure that you are using secure and private networks when accessing your Bitcoin-related accounts. Using Wi-Fi in a public place, for instance, is an opportunity for cyber thieves who can intercept unsecured data transmitted across such networks.

Another common pitfall in the Bitcoin sphere is falling victim to scams and phishing attempts. The cryptocurrency world, with its relative anonymity and significant financial stakes, is ripe for a variety of scams. Phishing attacks, where scammers attempt to trick you into giving them your personal information or login credentials, are particularly prevalent. Always double-check the URLs of sites you visit, and don't ever click on suspicious links from emails or messages. Be wary of too-good-to-be-true investment schemes that promise high returns with little to no risk. Remember, in the financial world, high returns always come with high risks, and this is especially true in the volatile cryptocurrency market. Educating yourself about common Bitcoin scams and staying informed about new threats can significantly reduce your risk of falling victim to cybercriminals.

Understanding the volatile nature of Bitcoin prices is crucial for every newcomer. The cryptocurrency market is known for its rapid price fluctuations, which can be exhilarating but also daunting. A common mistake is to make investment decisions based on panic or hype, which can lead to buying high and selling low—the opposite of the general investment strategy goal. Instead of reacting to market volatility with panic, a more measured approach involves doing thorough research and setting clear, strategic objectives for your investments. Decide how much of your portfolio you want to assign to Bitcoin and stick to this limit. It's also wise to avoid checking the price too frequently, which can prevent knee-jerk reactions to short-term market movements. Instead, focus on long-term trends and think about Bitcoin's potential in your investment portfolio.

Lastly, the legal and tax implications of owning and trading Bitcoin often go overlooked by beginners eager to dive into the market. The regulatory landscape for cryptocurrency is still evolving, and it varies significantly by country. Failing to comply with legal and tax obligations can involve serious consequences, including hefty fines and penalties. Take the time to understand the laws and regulations regarding Bitcoin in your jurisdiction. This might include reporting your transactions and holdings on your tax returns or adhering to specific legal guidelines about the use of cryptocurrency. Consulting with a financial advisor or a tax professional who is knowledgeable about cryptocurrency can provide you with tailored advice that will help you stay compliant and within the law.

By steering clear of these common mistakes, you can navigate the Bitcoin waters more safely and effectively. Remember, every step in managing your Bitcoin—from setting up your wallet to making informed investment decisions—should be approached with caution and knowledge. As you continue to learn and grow in your Bitcoin journey, these practices will not only protect your investments but also enrich your experience in the cryptocurrency world.

Verifying and Tracking Bitcoin Transactions

Understanding how to verify and track Bitcoin transactions is like learning to read the fine print of your financial activities, ensuring you're fully aware and in control. Each transaction on the Bitcoin network is recorded in a public ledger known as the blockchain. This transparency is Bitcoin's forte, allowing anyone to check the status of any transaction at any time. To verify a transaction, you can use a blockchain explorer. These are websites that provide detailed information about all transactions and blocks on the Bitcoin blockchain. By entering your transaction ID—a unique identifier assigned to each transaction—you can view its confirmation status and the number of times it has been confirmed by the network.

Confirmations are essential because they indicate how many blocks (additional transactions) have been added to the blockchain since your transaction was recorded. Generally, more confirmations mean higher security; most services require at least six confirmations for a transaction to be considered entirely secure.

Transaction fees play a pivotal role in the Bitcoin ecosystem, acting as an incentive for miners to include transactions in their blocks. These fees are not fixed and may vary widely depending on several factors, including the data size of the transaction and network demand. Higher fees may encourage faster confirmation during periods of congestion, as miners will prioritize transactions with higher fees. Deciding on an appropriate fee can sometimes feel like a balancing act. Most Bitcoin wallets provide a fee estimator that suggests a fee based on current network conditions and transaction size, which can guide you to set a fee that balances cost with confirmation speed. It's also helpful to check the current average transaction fees using a blockchain explorer or dedicated fee tracking websites to ensure you're not overpaying.

Keeping track of your Bitcoin holdings is crucial, especially as your portfolio grows. There are several tools and methods that can help with this, such as portfolio trackers and applications that allow you to monitor the value of your Bitcoin holdings in real time, along with other investments. Many of these trackers can link directly to your wallets and exchange accounts to automatically update your balances and transaction history. For those who prefer a more hands-on approach, accounting software that supports cryptocurrencies can be invaluable. These programs can help you record transactions, calculate gains and losses, and even prepare financial reports, thus simplifying the management of your Bitcoin finances.

Maintaining privacy in your Bitcoin transactions can be challenging but is crucial, especially given the public nature of the blockchain. One fundamental practice is to use a new address for each transaction. Most modern wallets automatically generate a new address for you for every transaction, which can help obscure which transactions are connected to you. For enhanced privacy, consider using a privacy-focused wallet or services that mix your Bitcoins with others, breaking the traceable path on the blockchain. However, be cautious with these services as they can sometimes operate in legally grey areas.

By mastering these aspects of Bitcoin transactions, you empower yourself with the knowledge to navigate the crypto waters safely, keeping your transactions secure, your fees appropriate, and your privacy intact. With these skills, you can confidently monitor and manage your digital assets, ensuring your Bitcoin journey is both rewarding and secure.

As we wrap up this chapter on getting started with Bitcoin, you've equipped yourself with the essential tools and knowledge to set up and secure a wallet, make educated purchases, understand the importance of private keys, and avoid common pitfalls. With this foundation, you're ready to delve deeper into the strategic aspects of Bitcoin investing, which we will explore in the next chapter. Here, we'll shift our focus from the mechanics of handling Bitcoin to making informed decisions that align with your financial goals.

Chapter 4

Investment Strategies and Managing Risks

Imagine stepping into the world of Bitcoin investing with a roadmap in your hands, one that not only shows you where to go but also when to take action. That's what this chapter aims to provide—a guide to understanding the rhythms and cues of the Bitcoin market that can significantly enhance your investing strategy. Let's start with a deep dive into the market cycles of Bitcoin, explore the impact of global events, and learn how to harness tools for sentiment analysis and timing techniques. These insights will not only bolster your confidence but will also refine your investing decisions, helping you to navigate the ups and downs of the market with greater ease.

Assessing the Right Time to Invest in Bitcoin

Understanding Market Cycles

The Bitcoin market experiences cycles that can provide insightful cues for investment decisions, like any other financial market. These cycles are characteristically composed of four phases: accumulation, uptrend, distribution, and downtrend. During the accumulation phase, prices are generally flat as knowledgeable investors begin to buy, anticipating future value increases. This phase is often marked by a sense of uncertainty among average investors. Next, the uptrend phase (also known as the 'markup' phase) begins, where prices start rising steadily and public interest grows. This is often where you'll see media buzz and hear stories of people making substantial gains.

Following the uptrend, the market enters the distribution phase. Here, traders and investors start to sell their holdings, taking profits from the increases during the uptrend. Prices may still rise on average, but fluctuations begin to appear, showing the first signs of volatility. Finally, the downtrend phase sets in, where prices fall, sometimes as dramatically as they rose. This can be generated by various factors, including market saturation, external economic factors, or a change in investor sentiment. Understanding these phases can help you recognize whether Bitcoin is currently undervalued or overpriced, guiding your decisions on when might be a good time to buy or sell.

Impact of Global Events

Global events significantly impact Bitcoin's price, reflecting its interconnection with worldwide economic and political landscapes. For instance, regulatory announcements regarding cryptocurrency, such as a new government policy to either support or restrict the use of Bitcoin, often lead to immediate and significant market reactions. Economic crises, trade wars, or geopolitical events can also influence Bitcoin prices. For example, during times of economic instability, such as the financial crisis in Greece in 2015, more people turned to Bitcoin, pushing prices up. On the other hand, announcements of regulatory crackdowns, such as those in China in 2017, can cause prices to plummet.

Sentiment Analysis

Sentiment analysis involves gauging the mood or opinions of the market participants, often through analyzing data from several sources, including social media, news articles, and market indicators. Tools like sentiment indicators or social media analytics software can help you tap into the market's mood and provide clues about potential price movements. For example, a sudden spike in negative sentiment on social media platforms can sometimes precede a drop in Bitcoin prices, as it may indicate growing investor anxiety or pessimism.

Timing Techniques

One effective strategy to manage investment timing in such a volatile market is dollar-cost averaging (DCA). This technique means investing a fixed amount at regular intervals in Bitcoin, regardless of the price—a strategy that will help reduce the impact of instability on the overall purchase. The idea is to build up the investment over time, smoothing out the purchasing price across the highs and lows of the market's cycle. Another timing technique is to buy during periods of consolidation—when prices are relatively stable—before the next market moves higher. This requires keeping a keen eye on market trends and being prepared to act when the time seems right.

Through understanding market cycles, the impact of global events, sentiment analysis, and strategic timing, you can improve your ability to make informed investment decisions in the Bitcoin market. These elements provide a framework within which you can assess the market's current condition and its potential future movements, helping you to buy and sell with greater confidence and theoretically better outcomes. As we navigate through these concepts, remember that investing in Bitcoin, like any investment, involves a degree of risk. The key is to make well-informed decisions, drawing on a broad range of tools and information to guide your investment strategy.

Long-term vs. Short-term Bitcoin Investment Strategies

When you step into the Bitcoin investment arena, it's like choosing between sprinting or running a marathon. Both styles have their unique rhythms and rewards, and knowing the nuances of each can significantly impact your financial outcome. First, let us define what long-term and short-term investments generally look like in the Bitcoin context. Long-term investment, often referred to as "HODLing" in the crypto community, means holding onto Bitcoin with the expectation that its value will increase over years or even decades. This strategy is less about daily fluctuations and more about the big picture, counting on the idea that despite its volatility, Bitcoin will continue to gain value over time. Short-term investment, on the other hand, is more like day trading, where investors buy and sell Bitcoin based on short-term market movements. These can last from a few minutes to several months, depending on the strategy.

The pros and cons of each are worth considering. Long-term holding has the potential for substantial returns, as history has shown significant price increases for Bitcoin over several years. This strategy requires less time and attention on a daily basis, as you won't be reacting to every dip or peak. However, this requires a lot of patience and a strong nerve to ride out the inevitable ups and downs. Emotional stress is often lower, as long-term investors are generally not swayed by short-term market volatility. On the flip side, short-term trading can also be lucrative, offering the possibility of profiting from Bitcoin's unpredictability by capitalizing on market highs and lows—a strategy that requires a deep understanding of market trends and a lot of time to monitor market movements. It can be highly stressful, as money can be lost as quickly as it was gained.

To bring these strategies to life, consider the real-life examples of two Bitcoin investors. Let's start with Sarah, a long-term holder who bought her first Bitcoin in 2014 when the price was around $800. Despite the dramatic fluctuations, including the peak near $20,000 in 2017 and the subsequent drop below $4,000 in 2018, she held onto her investment. By 2021, her patience paid off when the price soared to new heights, significantly increasing her initial investment. Contrast this with Mike, a short-term trader who started trading Bitcoin in late 2019. By carefully analyzing market trends and sentiment, he made multiple trades over weeks and months, capturing profits during the volatility of the 2020 and 2021 market surges. While both faced different challenges and stress levels, their tailored strategies worked well for each individual's financial goals and risk tolerances.

Choosing between these strategies involves a careful assessment of your financial goals, risk tolerance, and time availability. If you're looking at Bitcoin as a way to build wealth over many years, perhaps even as part of your retirement plan, then long-term investing might be for you. This approach will be less stressful as it doesn't require constant market monitoring. However, if you enjoy the thrill of trading and can afford the time and the emotional rollercoaster of short-term market movements, then short-term strategies might be more up your alley. It's also worth considering a mixed approach, where you hold a core amount of Bitcoin long-term but allocate a smaller portion for short-term trading.

When navigating through these investment strategies, remember that each investor's journey is unique. What works for one person might not work for another. The key is to understand the characteristic risks and benefits of each strategy and choose one that aligns with your financial goals and lifestyle. Whether you choose to sprint or run the marathon, or even a combination of both, the world of Bitcoin investing is ripe with opportunities for those who are prepared. As you explore these strategies, continue to refine your approach based on your experience and developing market conditions. This adaptive strategy can help ensure that your investment decisions are sound, responsive, and, in due course, more rewarding.

Risk Management in Bitcoin Investments

Navigating the turbulent waters of Bitcoin investing requires more than just knowing when to buy and sell. Effective risk management is crucial in order to safeguard your investment from the unexpected twists and turns in the cryptocurrency market. Let's unpack some fundamental risk management concepts that every Bitcoin investor should understand and implement.

Risk management in the context of Bitcoin investing involves strategic techniques to minimize potential losses while maximizing potential gains. One of the key concepts here is the risk/reward ratio, which helps you assess whether the potential reward of a Bitcoin investment outweighs the risk involved. This ratio is calculated by dividing the amount you will lose if the price moves against you (the risk) by the potential gain (the reward) if the price moves in your favor. A favorable risk/reward ratio is typically greater than 1:1, meaning the potential gains should outweigh the potential losses. Another vital concept is position sizing, which involves determining how much of your total investment capital to allocate to a particular investment. Proper position sizing is crucial as it helps you spread your risk and avoid significant damage from a single trade.

Additionally, using a stop-loss order can be a game changer. A stop-loss order is one placed with your broker to purchase or sell once the asset has reached a specific price. It is designed to limit an investor's loss on a position in a security. By placing a stop-loss order, you can automatically sell off your Bitcoin if its price dips to a level you have predefined as unacceptable, thus preventing further losses.

Identifying the risks associated with Bitcoin investing is just as critical as knowing how to manage them. Their volatility is perhaps the most well-known risk. The price of Bitcoin has been known to wildly fluctuate over short periods, influenced by factors such as market sentiment, regulatory news, and changes in the technological landscape. Regulatory changes are another significant risk. As governments around the world grapple with how to handle cryptocurrencies, new regulations can have sudden and profound effects on the market. For instance, an announcement of stricter regulations can lead to price drops, while favorable regulations can cause prices to surge. Technically, Bitcoin is not immune to vulnerabilities. The technology underlying Bitcoin is still relatively new, and unforeseen bugs or flaws in the system could potentially be exploited, leading to loss of funds.

Mitigating these risks starts with diversification. Don't put all your eggs in one basket! While Bitcoin might be the star of your portfolio, consider diversifying into other cryptocurrencies or blockchain projects to spread your risk. This move will protect your portfolio from being too exposed to the fortunes (or misfortunes) of a single asset. Using secure storage solutions is also paramount—use hardware wallets, which store your private keys offline and protect from computer viruses and hackers. Keeping yourself informed cannot be overstressed. Stay updated on technological and regulatory developments in the cryptocurrency world. This can help you to anticipate potential issues and adapt your strategy accordingly, possibly saving you from substantial losses.

Creating a personalized risk management plan involves several steps. Start by defining clear investment objectives. What are you hoping to achieve with your Bitcoin investment? Are you looking for short-term gains, or are you in it for the long haul? If you understand your goals, this will help you control how much risk you are willing to take. Next, assess your risk tolerance, which measures your willingness to endure the market's volatility and uncertainty. Your risk tolerance will certainly affect how much of your portfolio you might want to allocate to Bitcoin versus other less volatile investments. Once you have a clear understanding of your objectives and risk tolerance, establish mechanisms to monitor and adjust your investment plan as necessary. This will probably involve setting up regular reviews of your portfolio, keeping an eye on market developments, and being poised to adapt your strategy in response to new information.

By integrating these risk management techniques into your Bitcoin investing strategy, you can protect your investments from unexpected downturns and improve your chances of long-term success. Risk management will not eliminate risk entirely—that's impossible in any investment—but understand and manage the risks in a way that aligns with your overall investment goals. With a solid plan in place, you can approach Bitcoin investing with confidence, knowing that you are prepared to handle whatever the market throws your way.

Diversifying Your Investment Portfolio with Bitcoin

When you think about diversifying your investment portfolio, you're essentially looking at ways to spread out your investment risks and increase your potential for returns. This is where Bitcoin can play a pivotal role. As a non-correlated asset, Bitcoin has shown that its market movement is not typically aligned with traditional financial assets like stocks or bonds. This unique attribute makes it a valuable tool for diversification, helping to reduce overall investment risk while providing a hedge against inflation and economic instability. For instance, during times when traditional markets may be underperforming due to economic downturns or inflationary pressures, Bitcoin's price has sometimes moved independently or even appreciated, offering a buffer that can help stabilize your portfolio's value.

Diversifying within the cryptocurrency space itself can also enhance your investment strategy. Beyond Bitcoin, the world of cryptocurrencies is rich with alternatives, including various altcoins and tokens, each offering different technologies, use cases, and potential benefits. For example, Ethereum, with its smart contract functionality, presents a different set of opportunities and risks compared to Bitcoin. There are also stablecoins, which are pegged to traditional currencies like the US dollar, providing stability in a portfolio that includes more volatile crypto assets. Furthermore, the burgeoning field of DeFi, or decentralized finance, offers yield-generating opportunities through mechanisms such as staking, lending, and liquidity provision, which are not typically found in other traditional financial products.

Another layer of diversification can be achieved through Bitcoin derivatives, such as futures and options. These financial instruments allow you to hedge your bets or speculate on Bitcoin's price movements without actually holding the currency. For instance, if you believe Bitcoin's price will go down, you could buy a put option or sell a futures contract as a form of insurance against losses in your Bitcoin holdings. This strategy can be very useful in managing the risks associated with Bitcoin's price volatility.

Balancing traditional investments with cryptocurrency holdings is more of an art than a science. It involves understanding not only the potential returns and risks of each asset class but also how they interact within your overall portfolio. A well-rounded portfolio characteristically includes a mix of assets—stocks, bonds, real estate, and, increasingly, cryptocurrencies like Bitcoin. Each of these plays a role in achieving your financial goals, whether it's capital appreciation, income generation, or preservation of capital. For instance, bonds offer regular income and are generally safer, while stocks and Bitcoin may provide higher growth potential but with increased risk. Real estate offers tangible asset ownership and can also provide income through rent.

Monitoring and rebalancing your portfolio are crucial practices to make sure that your investments continue to align with your financial goals and risk tolerance. This involves regularly reviewing your asset allocation to confirm it remains optimal. For example, if Bitcoin's value has increased significantly, it might represent a larger proportion of your portfolio than you initially intended, increasing your overall risk. In such cases, you might decide to sell some of your Bitcoin to rebalance your portfolio back to its target allocation. Tools and platforms that provide comprehensive views of your assets and automated rebalancing can help simplify this process, allowing you to easily stay on top of your investments.

By incorporating Bitcoin and other cryptocurrencies into your diversified investment portfolio, you're not only spreading your risk but also positioning yourself to capitalize on the growth potential of some of the most dynamic and innovative asset classes in the market today. As with any other investment, the key to success lies in careful planning, ongoing education, and staying adaptable to the ever-changing financial landscape.

Using Technical Analysis to Guide Bitcoin Investments

As you dip your toes into the vast ocean of Bitcoin investing, understanding the currents—market trends and patterns—can significantly enhance your navigation skills. This is where technical analysis comes into play, serving as a compass to guide your investment decisions. Technical analysis primarily involves the study of price, volume, and past market data to forecast future price movements. This method is built on the assumption that all up-to-date market information is reflected in the price, which follows identifiable patterns or trends that are likely to repeat over time.

One of the basic concepts in technical analysis is the identification of trends. A trend can indicate the general direction in which the market is moving and can be upward, downward, or sideways. Recognizing these trends early can help you make decisions about when to buy or sell. For example, in a strong upward trend, it might be advantageous to hold onto your Bitcoin, whereas a downward trend might signal a good time to sell or wait for a more favorable entry point. Closely tied to trends are support and resistance levels, which are predetermined points on the price chart where the forces of supply and demand meet. Support levels are prices at which buyers consistently enter the market, preventing prices from further deterioration, while resistance levels are the prices at which the sellers repeatedly cap price increases.

The volume of trades is another critical indicator in technical analysis as it provides clues about the strength of a price move. High volumes often confirm the trend direction, as they suggest that a large number of assets are being traded. For instance, if the Bitcoin price breaks above a known resistance level on high volume, this is generally taken as a confirmation that the price might continue to rise as buyer interest is strong.

Several key indicators are invaluable to refine your technical analysis. Moving averages are among the most popular and easy-to-use tools. They streamline the price data to create a single flowing line, making it easier to identify the direction of the trend. The Simple Moving Average (SMA) and the Exponential Moving Average (EMA) are two types you might consider. The Relative Strength Index (RSI) is an additional powerful tool that can be used to calculate the speed and change of prices using a scale of 0 to 100—an asset is typically considered to be overbought when the RSI is above 70 and oversold when it's below 30, potentially signaling upcoming reversals. The Moving Average Convergence Divergence (MACD) is a more sophisticated tool that helps track momentum by displaying the relationship between two moving averages of a cryptocurrency's price. Lastly, Bollinger Bands provide a visual of the price volatility; they widen during periods of high volatility and contract when volatility decreases.

Chart patterns may also play a critical role in technical analysis, as they help traders predict future market movements. Patterns like the 'head and shoulders' or 'double top' can indicate trend reversals, while 'triangles' or 'flags' can signal the continuation of a trend. Being able to spot these patterns early will give you a substantial advantage in your trading strategy.

While technical analysis can be incredibly powerful, it's most effective when used in conjunction with fundamental analysis, which involves evaluating a cryptocurrency's value based on external factors and intrinsic value. This holistic type of approach can provide a more comprehensive view of the market, combining the 'what' and 'why' of market movements. For instance, if technical analysis suggests a bullish trend but recent regulatory changes are likely to impact the cryptocurrency negatively, it might be wise to temper your actions with this fundamental insight.

By mastering technical analysis, you equip yourself with the tools to make more informed decisions about your Bitcoin investments. This method won't guarantee success, as markets can be unpredictable, but it will provide a solid framework for understanding market dynamics and managing potential risks. As you grow more comfortable with these concepts, you'll find yourself better able to anticipate and react to market movements, potentially leading to more successful investment outcomes.

As we conclude this exploration of technical analysis, remember that the key to effective Bitcoin investing lies in a balanced approach that considers both market trends and underlying factors. The insights gained from technical analysis are valuable, but they are just one part of the broader investment landscape. Looking ahead, the next chapter delves into the exciting realm of Bitcoin technologies, where innovation continues to reshape the possibilities within the cryptocurrency world. This exploration will not only broaden your understanding of what drives Bitcoin but also enhance your ability to navigate its future developments.

Chapter 5

Advanced Bitcoin Technologies

Diving into the world of Bitcoin mining might feel like you're stepping into a digital gold rush era, where instead of shovels and pans, miners arm themselves with powerful computers and a sharp understanding of cryptography. This chapter will unravel the fascinating process of Bitcoin mining by exploring each step, from the role of miners to the sophisticated evolution of mining technology that keeps the Bitcoin network robust and secure.

An In-depth Look at Bitcoin Mining

Imagine a worldwide competition where millions of participants solve complex puzzles 24/7, and the winners get rewarded in digital gold—Bitcoin. This is Bitcoin mining in a nutshell, but let's break it down further to understand the intricacies involved. Mining is shown to be the backbone of the Bitcoin network. Miners utilize powerful computers to solve cryptographic puzzles, and the first to reach the solution may add a new block of transactions to the Bitcoin blockchain. This process not only creates new bitcoins but also verifies and secures transactions without the need for a central authority.

Mining Process Explained

The mining process begins when transactions are broadcast to the network. Miners collect these transactions and start forming a block.

Individual blocks contain a cryptographic hash of the preceding block, which links them in a chain, hence the term 'blockchain.' To add a block to a chain, the miner has to find the solution to a complex cryptographic puzzle related to the hash of the previous block. This puzzle involves guessing a number called a nonce. The correct nonce, combined with the data in the block, produces a hash that meets the network's required standards, known as the difficulty level. This level adjusts every 2016 blocks, roughly every two weeks, to ensure that the time to find a block remains about ten minutes, regardless of how many miners are competing.

Role of Mining Pools

Given the competitive nature of mining and the sheer computational power required, an individual miner often finds it challenging to compete with larger mining operations. This is where mining pools come into play—a group of miners who combine their computing power to increase their chances of solving cryptographic puzzles and earning rewards. When a pool succeeds, the reward is distributed among its members based on the amount of computing power each contributed. This collaboration makes mining more accessible to individuals who might not have the resources to mine alone, democratizing the process to some extent and ensuring that the network remains decentralized.

Impact on Network Security

Mining is not just about creating new coins; it's crucial for maintaining the security and integrity of the Bitcoin network. The process of cracking cryptographic puzzles to add new blocks acts as a deterrent against fraud and malicious attacks. Since altering any information on the blockchain would require redoing all the work of subsequent blocks, the computational effort (and thus the electricity and cost involved) needed to achieve such deceit is impractical. This built-in security mechanism is why Bitcoin remains remarkably secure despite its open and decentralized nature.

Evolution of Mining Technology

The technology behind Bitcoin mining has evolved significantly since Bitcoin's inception. Initially, miners used standard multi-core CPUs to mine Bitcoin. However, as the difficulty of the puzzles increased, the community discovered that graphics processing units (GPUs) were much more effective at solving Bitcoin's hashing puzzles. GPUs were followed by Field-Programmable Gate Arrays (FPGAs) and then Application-Specific Integrated Circuits (ASICs), each more powerful and energy-efficient than the last. ASICs are now the standard mining hardware for Bitcoin due to their ability to perform hash calculations at a much faster rate than CPUs or GPUs while also using less power. This evolution reflects the growing complexity and competitiveness of Bitcoin mining, but it also raises concerns about the increasing centralization of mining power in the hands of those who can afford these expensive technologies.

Reflection Section

As you delve deeper into the mechanics of Bitcoin mining, consider the balance between the democratizing potential of mining pools and the centralizing force of advanced mining technologies. Reflect on how these dynamics affect the overall security and distribution of power within the Bitcoin network. What are your thoughts on the sustainability of Bitcoin mining, considering the vast amount of energy it consumes? How do you see technological advancements shaping the future of mining?

Understanding the mining process provides a window into the technical wizardry that keeps Bitcoin secure and functional. As we explore further, the complexities of Bitcoin mining unfold, revealing not just a race for new coins but a robust mechanism that supports the entire Bitcoin ecosystem.

The Significance of Hash Rates in Mining

When stepping into the realm of Bitcoin mining, one term that frequently pops up is 'hash rate.' This might sound like something out of a complex math class, but it's actually a critical element in the mining process. Think of the hash rate as the horsepower of a car in the world of Bitcoin mining—it represents the mining power of the network. Specifically, hash rate refers to the number of calculations that a given network can perform each second. It's a vital metric that tells us about the health and the strength of the Bitcoin mining network. High hash rates mean more security and more efficiency, which are crucial in preventing attacks and processing transactions smoothly.

The relationship between the hash rate and mining difficulty is a dynamic interaction that ensures the stability of how new blocks are added to the blockchain. Mining difficulty adjusts approximately every two weeks or every 2016 blocks, which is designed to ensure that no matter how much mining power is added to the network, the average time to find a block remains about ten minutes. When more miners join the network and the hash rate increases, the puzzles become more difficult to solve. Conversely, if the hash rate drops, the puzzles become easier. This self-regulating mechanism maintains the pace of block creation, ensuring that despite fluctuations in miner participation, the blockchain's functionality and security remain intact.

Understanding the hash rate is not just about gauging the processing power. It also serves as a barometer for the security of the network. A higher hash rate means greater resistance to attacks, making it exponentially more difficult for any single entity to take control of the network or to alter the blockchain. This security is paramount, not just for the integrity of transactions but for the trust in the Bitcoin system as a whole. In essence, a robust hash rate protects the network from potential threats, including the notorious 51% attack, where an individual or group could potentially take control of the majority of the mining power and manipulate transaction confirmations.

The economic implications of hash rate fluctuations can be significant for miners. As the hash rate rises, the difficulty of mining also rises, requiring more computational power and, thus, more electricity. For miners, this means higher operational costs. When combined with the volatile price of Bitcoin, these factors can greatly influence profitability. Miners need to constantly assess the efficiency of their operations against the current hash rate and the price of Bitcoin. For instance, a sudden increase in hash rate without a corresponding rise in Bitcoin prices could reduce profit margins, pushing less efficient miners out of the market. Conversely, a decline in hash rate can lead to decreased difficulty levels, potentially making mining more profitable, especially if Bitcoin prices hold steady or increase.

Moreover, changes in the hash rate can affect transaction times and fees. During periods of low hash rates and network congestion, transactions can take longer to confirm, leading users to pay higher fees for quicker confirmations. This dynamic can influence user experience and the perception of Bitcoin's viability for daily transactions. On a broader scale, significant shifts in the hash rate could impact the entire Bitcoin market, influencing investor confidence and the cryptocurrency's price stability.

As you navigate through the complexities of Bitcoin mining, understanding the implications of hash rate is crucial. It not only affects your potential success as a miner but also impacts the broader Bitcoin network and market. By keeping a close eye on hash rate trends and adjusting your strategies accordingly, you can enhance your understanding and engagement with Bitcoin, making more informed decisions, whether you're mining, investing, or simply curious about how this groundbreaking technology operates.

Understanding Bitcoin's Algorithmic Framework

Peeling back the layers of Bitcoin's core, the SHA-256 algorithm emerges as a cornerstone of its cryptographic security. Developed by the National Security Agency (NSA) of the United States, SHA-256 stands for Secure Hash Algorithm 256-bit and is part of the SHA-2 family. It was selected for Bitcoin due to its solid security credentials and efficiency in processing. The primary role of SHA-256 in Bitcoin is to ensure that the data within the blockchain remains unaltered and secure. Every transaction and block in the Bitcoin network undergoes a SHA-256 transformation, which outputs a unique 256-bit signature for each. This signature acts as a digital fingerprint: unique, unrepeatable, and irreversible. If even a single character in a block is changed, the hash will change completely, signaling potential tampering to the network.

This hashing process is vital for maintaining the integrity and immutability of transactions. When a new block is created, its content is run through SHA-256, producing a hash that is then stored in the block header. This hash includes not only transactions but also the previous block's hash, creating a chain where each block is cryptographically linked to its predecessor. This linkage is what makes the blockchain immutable. To alter any information on a block, an attacker would need to recalibrate the hash not just for that block but for every subsequent block, a task that requires immense computational power and is, therefore, practically unfeasible. This cryptographic chaining defends the network against fraud and ensures that once a transaction is recorded in the blockchain, it is effectively impossible to alter.

Moving on to scalability, Bitcoin faces significant challenges as it grows. The SHA-256 algorithm is computationally intensive, and with the Bitcoin network limited to processing transactions in 1 MB blocks approximately every ten minutes, the system can handle only around 7 transactions per second (tps). In comparison, traditional systems like Visa can process thousands of tps. This limitation has led to bottlenecks and increased transaction fees, particularly during times of high demand. Several solutions have been proposed to address these issues. One notable attempt is the implementation of Segregated Witness (SegWit), which optimizes the space within each block by separating (or segregating) the transaction signatures (witnesses) from the transaction data. This segregation allows more transactions to fit within a block and improves the efficiency of transaction processing without altering the block size.

Looking forward, the Bitcoin community continues to explore potential adjustments to its algorithmic framework to better meet the evolving needs and challenges. One of the most significant concerns is quantum resistance. Quantum computing promises to bring vast improvements in processing power but also poses new risks to cryptographic systems like SHA-256. Although current quantum computers are not yet capable of breaking Bitcoin's cryptography, future advancements might make it possible. In response, there's ongoing research into post-quantum cryptographic algorithms that could potentially be integrated into Bitcoin's framework. These algorithms are designed to be secure against both classical and quantum computing threats, ensuring the long-term security of the network as computational technologies advance.

The continuous evolution of Bitcoin's algorithmic framework is a testament to the dynamic and innovative spirit of the Bitcoin community. As we navigate the complexities of cryptographic security, scalability challenges, and the looming advent of quantum computing, Bitcoin remains at the forefront of technological advancement in the cryptocurrency space. By understanding the underlying mechanisms that protect and power the network, we are able to appreciate not just the how of Bitcoin transactions but the why—why it remains secure, why it continues to attract attention, and why it stands as a pioneering force in the digital currency landscape.

Innovations in Bitcoin: Lightning Network and Beyond

When you think about using Bitcoin for everyday transactions— buying a cup of coffee, for example, the hesitation often comes from the wait times and fees associated with Bitcoin's blockchain. Enter the Lightning Network. This is a second-layer solution that operates on top of Bitcoin's existing blockchain, aiming to make transactions faster and more cost-effective. What this means for you is that Bitcoin can potentially handle transactions as quickly and inexpensively as swiping a credit card.

Introduction to the Lightning Network

The Lightning Network isn't just a minor tweak to how Bitcoin operates; it's an ambitious overhaul designed to combat the scalability issues that have been a significant concern for Bitcoin since its inception. By enabling a system where transactions don't need to be immediately broadcast to the blockchain, the Lightning Network dramatically reduces the load on the network. This is crucial because the current model, where every transaction is recorded on the blockchain, leads to congestion and increased transaction fees, which in turn make microtransactions or everyday purchases impractical with Bitcoin.

How the Lightning Network Works

Imagine you and a friend decide to set up a tab that allows you to make multiple transactions between each other throughout the day without settling up after every exchange. At the end of the day, only the net amount is settled. The Lightning Network works similarly but on a much larger scale. It allows two parties to open a payment channel between them that exists off the blockchain. Once this channel is open, they can exchange Bitcoin an unlimited number of times without committing these transactions to the Bitcoin blockchain right away. Only when the channel is closed will the final balances be broadcasted to the public blockchain. This method not only speeds up transactions but also significantly reduces transaction fees, as the need to record every transaction on the blockchain is eliminated.

The real magic happens when these channels interconnect with others, forming a network where you can send payments to someone even if you don't have a direct channel open with them.

The network automatically finds the shortest route through other connected channels. This interconnected network of channels greatly enhances Bitcoin's usability, making it not only possible but efficient for small, routine transactions.

Impact on Bitcoin Usability

The potential of the Lightning Network to enhance Bitcoin's usability for everyday transactions is vast. By shifting the transaction load off the main blockchain, Bitcoin can scale up to potentially millions of transactions per second—comparable to major credit card networks. This scalability makes using Bitcoin for small purchases, like a coffee or a book, not only possible but practical. It also opens up new avenues for Bitcoin in micropayments, such as tipping content creators or paying for articles on a per-view basis, avenues that were previously unfeasible due to high transaction costs and slow processing times.

Other Emerging Innovations

While the Lightning Network is one of the most promising innovations for addressing Bitcoin's limitations, it's not the only one. Sidechains and state channels are also pivotal in pushing Bitcoin's functionality forward. Sidechains are separate blockchains that are attached to the main Bitcoin blockchain. They allow for experimentation with new features without impacting the main chain. This can include features like smart contracts or different consensus mechanisms that make transactions faster or more secure.

State channels, similar to the Lightning Network, take the concept further by allowing not just Bitcoin transactions but any state changes to be conducted off the main blockchain. This could include changes in smart contracts or other forms of digital agreements.

These technologies collectively expand what's possible with Bitcoin, making it more versatile and adaptable to more wide-ranging uses beyond just a digital currency. By enhancing Bitcoin's functionality and addressing its limitations, these innovations not only improve its usability but also ensure its relevance in an increasingly competitive blockchain ecosystem.

Navigating through these advancements, it becomes evident that Bitcoin is much more than just digital gold; it's a growing, evolving technology that continuously adapts to meet the demands of its users. From making your daily coffee run smoother with the Lightning Network to exploring new digital agreements with state channels, the innovations surrounding Bitcoin are making it more accessible and functional for everyday use. As these technologies continue to evolve and integrate with the Bitcoin ecosystem, they pave the way for a future where Bitcoin's potential is fully unleashed, transforming not just how we view this cryptocurrency but also how we interact with the digital world at large.

Future Technologies Shaping Bitcoin

As we peer into the horizon of Bitcoin's technological evolution, several groundbreaking advancements in cryptography and hardware are ready to reshape its landscape. These developments not only promise enhanced security and efficiency but also allow for greater adoption and new functionalities. Among these, homomorphic encryption and zero-knowledge proofs stand out as frontrunners in the cryptographic arena, offering robust privacy enhancements that could revolutionize how transactions and data are managed in the Bitcoin network.

Homomorphic encryption is a form of cryptography that allows computations to be executed on encrypted data, returning encrypted results that, when decrypted, match the results of operations performed on the plaintext. This means that data can be processed without ever exposing it in its raw form, significantly enhancing data privacy and security. For Bitcoin, this could enable new forms of secure data processing and verification that won't compromise the privacy of transaction details. Imagine a scenario where you could verify the validity of a transaction or perform complex financial audits without ever revealing the underlying data—homomorphic encryption holds the key to this ability.

Zero-knowledge proofs present another fascinating area of cryptographic advancement. These are methods by which one party can prove to another that a given statement is true without conveying any additional information apart from the fact that the statement is indeed true. For Bitcoin, zero-knowledge proofs could greatly enhance transaction privacy by allowing users to verify transactions as valid without revealing anything about the transaction's inputs or outputs. This would be a momentous step forward in protecting financial privacy, enabling users to enjoy the benefits of public blockchain technology without exposing their financial activities.

Turning to blockchain interoperability, the seamless exchange of value and information across different blockchain systems is a pivotal development on the horizon. Interoperability can be thought of as the ability for different blockchain networks to communicate and transact without barriers, akin to how email systems work across different hosting platforms. For Bitcoin, enhancing interoperability means that it could more easily connect with other blockchains, opening a myriad of possibilities for cross-chain collaborations and functionalities. This could facilitate everything from multi-chain asset transfers to complex smart contracts that operate across different networks, broadening Bitcoin's utility and appeal.

Advancements in mining hardware also continue to shape Bitcoin's future. The next generation of mining hardware may focus on energy efficiency and accessibility, reducing the environmental impact of Bitcoin mining and making it more accessible to average users. This could involve the development of new types of mining chips that consume less power or the use of renewable energy sources to power mining operations. Such innovations would not only make Bitcoin mining more sustainable but also allow the mining process to be available to more people, ensuring that it remains in the hands of the many rather than the few.

Lastly, the potential impact of quantum computing looms large as a disruptive force in the realm of Bitcoin. A quantum computer, with its ability to solve complex mathematical problems at unprecedented speeds, could theoretically break Bitcoin's cryptographic security. However, the Bitcoin community is proactive, with ongoing research into quantum-resistant cryptographic methods that could safeguard Bitcoin against even the most advanced computational abilities. By staying ahead of these technological curves, Bitcoin is not just reacting to emerging threats but is preparing to thrive in the next wave of technological evolution.

As we wrap up this exploration of future technologies shaping Bitcoin, it's clear that the landscape of digital currencies is anything but static. From enhancing security and privacy with advanced cryptography to fostering seamless interactions across blockchain networks and pushing the frontiers of mining technology, Bitcoin continues to evolve. These advancements are not just technical upgrades; they are transformative shifts that could redefine the global financial landscape, making it more secure, efficient, and inclusive. As we turn the page to the next chapter, the ongoing innovation in Bitcoin technology promises to keep us on the edge of our seats, watching as the future of finance unfolds before our eyes.

Chapter 6

Legal and Regulatory Aspects

Imagine stepping into a vibrant market where every stall offers something different. Now, envision that each of these stalls represents a country with its own set of rules on what can be sold and how. This is quite similar to the diverse and colorful landscape of Bitcoin's legal and regulatory status across the globe. As you delve into the world of Bitcoin, understanding this complex tapestry of laws and regulations is crucial, not just to navigate safely but to maximize your opportunities and protect your investments.

Navigating Bitcoin's Legal Landscape

Legal Status of Bitcoin

The legal recognition of Bitcoin varies dramatically from one country to another, painting a global picture that can seem as varied as the weather. In some places, Bitcoin is embraced warmly, like in Japan, where it's recognized as a legal method of payment. Contrast this with countries like Algeria, where Bitcoin is banned outright. Then there are nations like the United States and Canada, where Bitcoin is not considered legal tender but is recognized as a commodity or taxable asset. This classification impacts everything from how Bitcoin is traded to how it's taxed, making an understanding of regional legal distinctions essential for anyone engaged in Bitcoin transactions.

Regulatory Bodies Involved

As Bitcoin does not respect national borders, various international regulatory bodies have stepped in to provide guidelines and oversight. In the United States, for example, the Securities and Exchange Commission (SEC) plays a pivotal role in regulating cryptocurrencies deemed as securities. Meanwhile, the Commodity Futures Trading Commission (CFTC) considers Bitcoin a commodity, influencing how it's traded. The UK's Financial Conduct Authority (FCA) oversees the trading of cryptocurrencies, ensuring fair practices and the protection of traders. Each of these bodies has a significant impact on the market dynamic and operational practices surrounding Bitcoin, shaping the environment in which you trade and invest.

Compliance Requirements

Diving deeper into the mechanics of regulatory compliance, two critical protocols come to the forefront: Anti-Money Laundering (AML) and Know Your Customer (KYC). These protocols are not just bureaucratic red tape; they are essential safeguards designed to avoid illegal actions such as money laundering and the financing of terrorism. Compliance with AML involves monitoring and reporting suspicious activities, while KYC focuses on verifying the identity of individuals to prevent fraud. For you, the investor or user, this means undergoing identity verification processes when signing up with exchanges or wallets, ensuring that your activities remain transparent and within the bounds of legal frameworks.

Legal Challenges and Litigations

The path of Bitcoin through the legal landscape hasn't been smooth. Various legal challenges and litigations have tested the resilience and adaptability of this digital currency. Notable among these is the SEC's lawsuit against Ripple Labs, alleging that its XRP tokens were sold as unregistered securities. Such cases not only affect the parties involved but also set precedents that shape future regulatory decisions and market practices. For you, keeping an eye on these developments is crucial, as they could influence market sentiment and regulatory trends, impacting your Bitcoin holdings and strategies.

Reflective Exercise: Understanding Your Legal Environment

To further solidify your understanding of Bitcoin's legal landscape, take a moment to reflect on the following:

- How does the legal status of Bitcoin in your country impact your ability to buy, sell, or use Bitcoin?

- Are you aware of the primary regulatory body overseeing cryptocurrencies in your region?

- Have you encountered any challenges with AML and KYC compliance in your Bitcoin transactions?

This exercise isn't just academic—it's a practical step towards becoming a savvy participant in the global Bitcoin market, equipped with the knowledge to navigate complex legal terrains confidently.

Global Regulations on Cryptocurrencies: An Overview

In the dynamic world of cryptocurrencies, the regulatory landscape is as varied as the technology itself, with different countries adopting distinct approaches based on their economic policies, culture, and understanding of digital currencies. Broadly speaking, these regulatory frameworks can be categorized into three types: permissive, contentious, and restrictive. Each of these regimes not only reflects the country's posture towards digital innovation and financial security but also significantly influences the adoption and development of cryptocurrencies like Bitcoin within their borders.

Starting with permissive jurisdictions, these are countries that have embraced the potential of cryptocurrencies by implementing friendly regulations that foster growth and innovation. A prime example is Japan, one of the first major economies to recognize Bitcoin as a legal payment method. This acknowledgment came in April 2017, when the Japanese government amended its Payment Services Act to bring cryptocurrency exchanges under regulatory scrutiny while ensuring they adhered to vigorous standards for security and compliance. This move was largely seen as a response to the infamous Mt. Gox incident, which highlighted the need for regulation to build trust and protect consumers. The result of this regulatory clarity has been overwhelmingly positive, leading to a surge in adoption both among consumers and businesses, with Japan often seen as a global leader in the cryptocurrency space.

In stark contrast are the contentious regimes, where the regulatory environment is mixed or uncertain, often with ongoing debates about how to approach cryptocurrencies. The United States is a quintessential example of this category. While not outright hostile, the U.S. presents a complex patchwork of regulations that vary by state and the nature of the cryptocurrency activity. For example, the Securities and Exchange Commission (SEC) is actively involved in determining whether certain cryptocurrencies qualify as securities, which would make them subject to stringent regulations. This ongoing uncertainty can stifle innovation and deter new participants due to fears of unexpected regulatory clampdowns. However, it also reflects a cautious approach aimed at balancing the potential risks and benefits of cryptocurrencies, protecting investors while trying not to hinder technological advancements.

On the more restrictive end of the spectrum are countries like China, which have taken a firm stance against the decentralized nature of cryptocurrencies and, in 2017, banned cryptocurrency exchanges and Initial Coin Offerings (ICOs) because of concern about the financial risks and potential for fraud associated with unregulated markets. More recently, in 2021, China extended this ban to include all cryptocurrency transactions and mining activities, quoting concerns over financial stability and environmental impact. This crackdown reflects China's broader strategy of controlling capital flows and maintaining the integrity of its financial system while also paving the way for the introduction of its digital currency, the Digital Yuan. The impact of these restrictive measures has been profound, leading to a significant drop in trading volumes within China and a migration of cryptocurrency businesses and miners to more crypto-friendly countries.

Amidst these diverse national approaches, international regulatory bodies, such as the Financial Action Task Force (FATF), perform a crucial role in shaping a cohesive global response to the challenges posed by cryptocurrencies. The FATF has developed guidelines that recommend measures for combating money laundering and terrorist financing associated with cryptocurrencies. These guidelines encourage countries to adopt regulatory practices that ensure that cryptocurrencies are not used for illicit activities while supporting innovation and financial inclusion. The FATF's efforts represent an attempt to bring a degree of harmonization to global cryptocurrency regulations, facilitating international cooperation and reducing the risk of regulatory arbitrage, where entities might move operations to jurisdictions with looser regulations.

Navigating this multifaceted regulatory landscape requires vigilance and adaptability. For you, as a participant in the cryptocurrency market, understanding the regulatory environment in each country where you operate is crucial. It not only helps you comply with the law but also helps you make informed decisions about where and how to conduct your cryptocurrency activities. Whether you're a casual investor, a serious trader, or a business leveraging cryptocurrency technology, staying informed about these regulations can help mitigate risks and capitalize on opportunities in the ever-evolving world of digital currencies.

Tax Implications for Bitcoin Investors

Navigating the tax implications of Bitcoin investments can seem like finding your way through a labyrinth, especially given the variations in tax treatment across different jurisdictions. When it comes to taxes, Bitcoin doesn't quite fit neatly into any traditional category—it's treated differently depending on where you are in the world. For example, in the United States, the Internal Revenue Service (IRS) classifies Bitcoin as property, not currency. This means that, much like owning real estate, any gain from the sale or exchange of Bitcoin is taxed as capital gains. This treatment aligns with how stocks and bonds are handled, where the purchase price (or basis) and the price at the time of sale determine the capital gain or loss reported on tax returns.

The specifics of reporting these transactions can be quite meticulous. In the U.S., every transaction involving Bitcoin, whether it's buying a cup of coffee or trading for another digital currency, must be reported on your tax returns. To do this effectively, maintaining thorough records of all your transactions is crucial—tracking the date of each transaction, the amount of Bitcoin involved, the value of Bitcoin at the time of the transaction, and the purpose of the transaction. This level of detail is necessary to accurately calculate any gains or losses, which are reported on Form 8949 and summarized on Schedule D of your tax return. The responsibility is on you to keep detailed records, as failing to report income, even unintentionally, can lead to penalties and interest.

For Bitcoin investors looking to optimize their tax situation, several strategies can be employed. Timing your disposals, for instance, can significantly impact your tax liability. In many places, the rate of tax you'll pay on capital gains can depend on how long you've held an asset. Typically, assets held for longer than a year may qualify for lower tax rates on gains in many jurisdictions. Another helpful strategy is tax-loss harvesting, where you sell Bitcoin at a loss to offset a capital gains tax liability. This can be especially helpful in a volatile market where values fluctuate widely. However, if you wish to claim the loss as a tax deduction, it's essential to be aware of the wash-sale rule, which prohibits the repurchase of the same or substantially identical asset within a 30-day period before or after it's sold at a loss.

Despite these strategies, one common pitfall that many Bitcoin investors fall into is failing to report their investments and transactions. Whether from misunderstanding the requirements or underestimating the implications of their activities, these oversights can lead to significant issues with tax authorities. In some cases, if the omission is found to be willful, it could even result in criminal charges. The key to avoiding such outcomes is straightforward: ensure compliance by staying informed about the tax regulations that apply to your Bitcoin activities and keeping meticulous records of all transactions.

Understanding and navigating the tax implications of Bitcoin investing are critical components of managing your investments wisely. By staying informed about them in your jurisdiction, diligently reporting all transactions, and employing strategies to manage tax liabilities, you can help ensure that your Bitcoin journey is both profitable and compliant. This proactive approach not only helps in optimizing your returns but also in maintaining a good standing with tax authorities, safeguarding your financial future in the evolving world of digital currencies.

Keeping Up with Regulatory Changes in Bitcoin

In the ever-evolving landscape of Bitcoin, staying informed about regulatory changes is not just beneficial—it's essential. Think of it as keeping a weather eye on the horizon; knowing when a storm is brewing or when clear skies can significantly alter your course and decisions. For those invested in Bitcoin, whether you're dabbling in mining, trading, or using it as a payment method, understanding the regulatory environment is crucial. Reliable sources for tracking these changes include government websites like the U.S. Securities and Exchange Commission or the Financial Conduct Authority in the UK. These sites often provide direct insights into current regulations and any forthcoming changes. Additionally, industry news outlets such as CoinDesk or The Block are invaluable for their timely and detailed analyses of how regulatory shifts across the globe could impact Bitcoin.

Moreover, any regulatory changes can have a profound impact on Bitcoin's market dynamics and investment strategies. For instance, a new regulation that affects how Bitcoin is mined could change the entire economic model for miners, influencing everything from the price of Bitcoin to its environmental impact. Similarly, changes in how Bitcoin is classified by financial authorities (think property vs. currency vs. commodity) can affect everything from your tax obligations to how you can use Bitcoin in your business operations. By staying informed, you can anticipate these changes, adjust your strategies accordingly, and ensure that you remain compliant and your investments are secure.

Engagement with regulatory bodies is another crucial element often overlooked by casual participants in the Bitcoin ecosystem. It's easy to think of regulation as something that happens 'to' us, but in reality, it's a dialogue. Participating in this dialogue can help shape policies that are fair and knowledgeable of the benefits of Bitcoin. Many regulatory bodies are open to feedback and often hold consultations with stakeholders before finalizing regulations. Getting involved in these discussions, either directly or through industry associations, can help ensure that the regulatory environment evolves in a way that supports innovation while protecting users.

Lastly, preparing for compliance involves more than just passively watching the regulatory landscape; it requires active preparation and adaptation. This might mean consulting with legal experts who specialize in cryptocurrency to understand how new regulations affect your particular situation. It also means implementing systems and processes that allow you to remain flexible and responsive to change. For businesses, this could involve developing compliance protocols that are easy to update as regulations change. For individual investors, it might mean setting up alerts or dedicating time each week to review the latest regulatory news.

Navigating the regulatory changes in Bitcoin doesn't have to be a daunting task. By leveraging reliable sources for information, understanding the potential impacts of regulatory shifts, engaging with policymakers, and preparing for compliance, you can ensure that you not only stay within the legal boundaries but also use these regulations to your advantage. As we close this chapter, remember that the landscape of Bitcoin regulation is continuously shaping the future of cryptocurrency. By staying informed and engaged, you equip yourself with the knowledge and tools needed to navigate this dynamic terrain successfully. As we move forward, the insights gained here will be invaluable in exploring the security aspects of Bitcoin in the next chapter, ensuring that your journey in cryptocurrency is secure and compliant.

Chapter 7

Security and Safety in Bitcoin Investment

Best Practices for Bitcoin Security

Imagine you've just stepped into the role of a digital bank vault manager, where every decision you make directly influences the safety and security of not just your assets but also those of others who trust your judgment. This scenario isn't far from reality when you dive into the world of Bitcoin investment. Here, every security measure you implement acts as a robust line of defense against potential threats. Let's explore some essential practices that are akin to setting up advanced, multi-layered security protocols for your digital vault.

Multi-Factor Authentication (MFA)

One of the first and most crucial steps in fortifying your Bitcoin security is enabling Multi-Factor Authentication (MFA) on all cryptocurrency-related accounts. Think of MFA as a series of different locks on your vault, where a thief would need to bypass not just one but multiple security checks. Typically, MFA combines something you know (like a password), something you have (like a smartphone for receiving a verification code), and something you are (like your fingerprint). By activating MFA, you significantly reduce the risk of unauthorized access, even if one of your security factors is compromised. This added layer effectively blocks intruders at multiple checkpoints, ensuring that accessing your digital funds is no easy feat.

Cold Storage Solutions

As you probe deeper into Bitcoin security, you'll encounter the concept of 'cold storage'—an effective method to keep your digital currency offline and out of reach from online threats. Cold storage solutions, hardware wallets, for example, are physical devices that store your Bitcoins away from the internet. These devices can be as small as a USB stick but come fortified with highly sophisticated security measures designed to protect your private keys—the digital codes that permit you to spend your Bitcoins. Unlike 'hot wallets' (Bitcoin wallets connected to the internet), hardware wallets are immune to viruses and remote hacking attempts, making them one of the safest options for the long-term storage of substantial Bitcoin holdings. Think of these as high-security vaults buried in a mountain, accessible only to you and impervious to external threats.

Secure Internet Practices

Navigating the internet without adequate protection can be likened to walking blindfold through a minefield. When managing Bitcoin transactions, it's critical to adopt secure internet practices to safeguard your digital assets. This includes using Virtual Private Networks (VPNs) that encrypt your internet connection, hiding your data flow from prying eyes, and protecting your anonymity online. Additionally, steer clear of public Wi-Fi networks when conducting transactions or accessing your Bitcoin wallet. Public networks are often less secure and can be breeding grounds for cyber threats like 'man-in-the-middle' attacks, where attackers intercept data being transferred over the network. By sticking to private, secured networks, you ensure that your Bitcoin transactions remain confidential and protected from unauthorized interceptions.

Regular Software Updates

Keeping your software updated is akin to regularly renovating and reinforcing your digital vault's walls. Software updates often include patches for security vulnerabilities that could be exploited by hackers. This includes updating your Bitcoin wallet software, antivirus programs, and even the operating system of the devices you use for your Bitcoin transactions. Each update not only enhances features but also strengthens security, closing off chinks in your digital armor that could be exploited by new strains of malware or hacking tactics. In the fast-evolving world of technology, staying updated is staying protected.

Reflective Exercise: Check Your Security Setup

To further solidify your understanding and application of these security practices, take a moment to assess your current Bitcoin security setup:

- Have you enabled MFA on all your cryptocurrency accounts?

- Are you using a cold storage option for your significant Bitcoin holdings?

- Do you consistently use secure and private internet connections for your transactions?

- When was the last time you updated your software and security programs?

This exercise is crucial in identifying any potential vulnerabilities in your security setup and underscores the importance of proactive measures in safeguarding your investments. As you continue to navigate the complex world of Bitcoin, remember that the security of your digital assets is paramount, and maintaining rigorous security practices is not just recommended; it's essential.

Recognizing and Avoiding Cryptocurrency Scams

Venturing into the world of cryptocurrency can sometimes feel like navigating a bustling marketplace, where amid the legitimate vendors, there are also hawkers peddling counterfeit goods. The excitement and potential for profit can sometimes overshadow the need for caution, making it easy to fall prey to scams designed to exploit the unwary. In this landscape, being able to recognize common scams and understanding how to verify the legitimacy of cryptocurrency offers become essential skills for safeguarding your digital assets.

One widespread type of scam in the cryptocurrency space is the phishing attack, where scammers attempt to trick you into giving away sensitive information, such as your wallet's private keys or login details to your exchange account. These attacks often come in the form of an email or website that looks almost identical to a legitimate service you might use, complete with logos and branding. However, the devil is in the details—perhaps the email address is slightly off, or the website URL has a subtle misspelling. Falling for this scam can lead to unauthorized access of your cryptocurrency holdings, essentially handing over the keys of your digital vault to a thief.

Another common scheme is the fake Initial Coin Offering (ICO), where scammers create a convincing pitch about a new cryptocurrency or blockchain project. They'll set up sleek websites and populate them with complex whitepapers and impressive team bios, often stolen from legitimate projects or entirely fabricated. The allure here is the promise of getting in on the ground floor of a new coin that could potentially offer high returns. However, once they've collected enough investment from unsuspecting backers, these fraudulent operators vanish, leaving investors with worthless tokens.

Ponzi schemes are also rampant in the crypto world. These scams promise high returns on your investment through strategies that are vague or secretive, asserting that profits are generated through revolutionary trading or mining techniques. However, the returns are not actually derived from any legitimate business activities but rather from the funds contributed by new investors. Once the inflow of new investors dries up, the scheme collapses, with most participants losing their money.

To shield yourself from such deceptive practices, it's crucial to recognize the red flags. Promises of guaranteed returns should always raise eyebrows. The volatile nature of cryptocurrencies makes it impossible to guarantee profits, so such promises are practically a hallmark of a scam. Similarly, if details about the project are sketchy or unverifiable, or if you're pressured to invest quickly, it's wise to step back and reconsider. High-pressure tactics are designed to override your better judgment by creating a sense of urgency that isn't really there.

When considering an investment, always take the time to do your homework. Start by researching the developers behind the project. Are their identities transparent? Do they have a track record or digital footprint that can be verified? Critically reading the project's whitepaper is another essential step. Does it lay out a clear, feasible plan, or is it filled with buzzwords that sound impressive but offer little real substance? Also, look for endorsements from reputable sources within the cryptocurrency community. If respected figures or entities are willing to associate their names with the project, it adds a layer of credibility.

If you ever suspect that you've been targeted by a scam, taking swift action can help mitigate potential damages. This includes reporting the incident to the relevant authorities, such as the Internet Crime Complaint Center (IC3) or the Federal Trade Commission (FTC) in the United States. Additionally, alert the cryptocurrency exchange or wallet service you use, as they may be able to assist in securing your accounts or even recovering lost funds. While the recovery of lost funds isn't guaranteed, especially in cases involving cryptocurrencies, promptly reporting the scam can prevent further losses and help authorities crack down on scammers.

Navigating the cryptocurrency landscape requires both enthusiasm for new technology and a healthy dose of skepticism. By staying informed and vigilant, you can protect yourself from scams and focus on the genuine prospects that the world of digital currencies can offer. Remember, the most powerful tool at your disposal is knowledge, and taking the time to acquire and apply this knowledge is your best defense in the dynamic and often murky waters of cryptocurrency investment.

The Role of Encryption in Securing Bitcoin Transactions

Diving into the realm of Bitcoin, the backbone supporting its robust security framework is cryptography, a sophisticated method of protecting information by transforming it into a secure format. This process, known as encryption, is pivotal in safeguarding your Bitcoin transactions from prying eyes and ensuring they are not tampered with during transmission or storage. Let's break down these cryptographic techniques to understand how they create a fortress around your Bitcoin dealings.

Cryptography in Bitcoin utilizes a specific type of algorithm known as SHA-256, which is part of a larger family of cryptographic hash functions. Think of a hash function as a way of taking an input (or 'message') and returning a fixed-size string of bytes. The output, typically a 'digest,' is exclusive to each unique input, and it changes significantly even with a tiny alteration in input. This characteristic ensures that any attempt to alter transaction data in any way will result in a different hash value, signaling an alert to the network about potential tampering. These hash functions make the history of Bitcoin transactions immutable, meaning once a transaction is recorded on the blockchain, it cannot be changed without altering all subsequent blocks and achieving consensus from the network—a task so computationally intensive that it becomes unfeasible in practice.

Venturing further into the cryptographic landscape of Bitcoin, we encounter the critical role played by public and private key encryption. In this system, each Bitcoin wallet has a 'public key,' which you can think of as an address that others can see and send Bitcoin to, and a 'private key,' which is known only to the wallet's owner. The private key is used to digitally sign transactions, providing mathematical proof that the transaction has come from the owner of that wallet. This signature, which is sent to the network for verification, ensures that the transaction is secure and the sender is authenticated. The beauty of this system lies in its simplicity and effectiveness. While the public key is visible to everyone on the network, the private key remains confidential, ensuring that only the owner can initiate transactions from their wallet. Therefore, safeguarding your private keys is akin to holding the keys to your safe—losing them means losing access to your Bitcoin.

To enhance transaction security further, advanced practices such as the use of multi-signature addresses have been developed. These require multiple parties to sign a transaction before it can be executed. This method is particularly useful in scenarios where you need to ensure that multiple stakeholders have approved a transaction, which adds an extra layer of security by distributing the permission to transact. You should also perform regular security audits of wallet platforms to help identify and mitigate potential vulnerabilities, ensuring that the wallet's infrastructure remains secure against evolving threats. These audits, performed by cybersecurity experts, examine everything from the software code to the user interface, ensuring that the wallet adheres to best security practices and that any potential security loopholes are closed.

Looking ahead, the horizon of cryptographic technologies holds promising developments that could further bolster the security of Bitcoin transactions. One of the most anticipated advancements is the development of quantum-resistant algorithms. With the advent of quantum computing, traditional cryptographic techniques could potentially be broken, exposing Bitcoin transactions to new types of threats. However, the Bitcoin community and researchers are already working on developing new types of encryption that can withstand the power of quantum computing. These future-proof cryptographic approaches aim to ensure that Bitcoin remains secure, even as the underlying technologies evolve.

Understanding these cryptographic principles and practices not only equips you with the knowledge to secure your Bitcoin transactions but also deepens your appreciation of the ingenuity behind Bitcoin's security model. As you continue to explore Bitcoin and engage in transactions, remember that the power of cryptography is a central pillar upholding the security and integrity of this digital currency. By staying informed about these techniques and the latest developments in the field, you can navigate the Bitcoin landscape with confidence, assured in the security of your transactions.

Backup and Recovery Solutions for Bitcoin Investors

When you're investing in Bitcoin, think of your digital assets as precious heirlooms in a family safe. Just as you'd secure and backup important family documents, your Bitcoin also requires a robust protection strategy—a strategy that ensures your digital wealth is safely backed up and recoverable in any eventuality. Let's delve into why backups are the cornerstone of digital asset security and how you can effectively safeguard your Bitcoin investments.

Importance of Backup

Imagine waking up one day to find that your digital wallet, holding all your Bitcoin, has become inaccessible or, worse, compromised. Without a backup, this scenario could mean a total loss of all your digital assets. This is where the importance of having strong backup solutions cannot be overstressed. Backups serve as a fail-safe, a way to restore your Bitcoin wallet if your primary access is lost due to device failure, theft, or a cyber attack. By maintaining a current backup, you ensure that you retain access to your funds under any circumstances. The key here is redundancy; having multiple backups in diverse forms and locations enhances the security and accessibility of your assets.

Digital vs. Physical Backups

In the realm of Bitcoin, backups can generally be categorized into two types: digital and physical. Digital backups, such as those stored on USB drives or external hard drives, offer convenience and quick access. They can be encrypted and stored in multiple locations, such as safe deposit boxes or secure cloud storage services that allow for encrypted data uploads. However, be aware that digital backups also carry the risk of being corrupted by malware or targeted by cyberattacks if not properly secured.

On the other hand, physical backups, such as paper wallets or metallic backups (where recovery phrases are engraved on metal for durability), provide an entirely offline option that completely eliminates the risk of online threats. These backups, however, are susceptible to physical hazards like fire, water damage, or even being misplaced. For the utmost security, it's prudent to use a combination of both digital and physical backups, leveraging the strengths of each to safeguard your investment.

Secure Backup Practices

To ensure the effectiveness of your backups, follow these best practices: First, utilize encrypted storage media for digital backups. Encryption adds an additional layer of security, making it difficult for unauthorized users to access your data even if they physically possess your backup device. Second, diversify the locations of your backups. This could mean keeping a USB drive in a safe at home, another in a safe deposit box at a bank, and perhaps a third with a trusted family member in a different geographic location. This strategy protects against the loss of your Bitcoin due to local disasters or theft.

Additionally, consider the use of tamper-evident bags or safes for physical backups. These can provide visible evidence if someone has attempted to access them, adding an extra layer of security. Regularly update your backups, especially after every transaction or when changes are made to your wallet's security settings. This ensures that the backup is current and all recent transactions are preserved.

Recovery Process

If the need arises to recover your Bitcoin wallet using your backup, the process should be approached with caution to avoid compromising your security. Begin by ensuring that the device or system you are using for recovery is secure and free of malware. Install a fresh, trusted version of your wallet software and prepare to enter your recovery phrase. This phrase, usually consisting of 12 to 24 words, acts as the key to restoring your wallet and its contents.

During recovery, it's crucial to enter the recovery phrase exactly as it was generated. Any mistake in transcription can prevent access to your funds. Once the wallet is restored, immediately create a new backup of the recovery phrase and consider transferring your funds to a new wallet with a freshly generated private key and recovery phrase. This move is especially recommended if you suspect that your previous wallet might have been compromised in any way.

By adhering to these backup and recovery protocols, you can be sure that your Bitcoin investments remain secure and accessible, no matter what challenges you might face. Regularly revisiting and updating your backup strategy is also crucial, as it keeps you prepared and responsive to the ever-evolving landscape of digital security threats. Remember, in the world of Bitcoin, proactive measures are the best defense against potential losses.

The Future of Cryptocurrency Security

As we navigate the developing landscape of cryptocurrency, it's clear that the frontier of digital security is expanding rapidly, introducing innovative technologies and practices that promise to redefine how we protect our digital assets. Among these advancements, biometric security systems stand out as a particularly promising development. Biometric systems use unique physical characteristics, such as fingerprints, iris patterns, or even facial recognition, to authenticate identity. This method could significantly enhance the security of cryptocurrency wallets and transactions by ensuring that access is strictly tied to the verified user. Imagine a world where accessing your digital wallet is as simple and secure as looking into a device that scans your iris. This technology isn't just futuristic—it's becoming increasingly practical and is poised to set new standards in securing personal and financial data.

Another intriguing area of development is decentralized identity verification, which leverages blockchain technology to create a secure, immutable identity for each user. This method could revolutionize security by making it exceedingly difficult for anyone to steal your identity. In a decentralized system, your identity isn't stored in a central database that is vulnerable to breaches. Instead, it's spread across a blockchain, accessible only through complex cryptographic protocols. This approach not only enhances security but also preserves privacy, giving you control over who can access your personal information and how it's used.

As these technologies develop, we must also consider the impact of regulatory changes within the cryptocurrency industry. Regulatory bodies worldwide are beginning to recognize the need for updated standards and compliance requirements to address the unique challenges that are posed by digital currencies. These changes could introduce new security protocols, such as stricter verification processes or mandatory compliance checks, which could, in turn, foster a safer trading environment. However, these regulations will need to strike a balance between enhancing security and preserving the innovation and accessibility that make cryptocurrencies unique.

Moreover, the role of education and community engagement in improving security cannot be overstated. As the cryptocurrency landscape grows, so does the need for comprehensive education on safe investment and trading practices. Community-driven initiatives and educational programs can play a crucial role in raising awareness about security best practices and emerging threats. By fostering a well-informed community, we can create a collective defense against scams, hacks, and other security threats, making the cryptocurrency ecosystem safer for everyone.

Looking ahead, we must also prepare for new threats that could challenge the security of our digital assets. Advanced phishing attacks and AI-driven hacking attempts are on the rise, employing increasingly sophisticated techniques to access secure information. These threats require us to be proactive and vigilant, constantly updating our security practices and staying informed about the latest cybersecurity developments. Preparing for these threats means not only adopting the latest security technologies but also anticipating potential vulnerabilities and responding swiftly to threats as they arise.

As we close this chapter on security and safety in Bitcoin investment, it's clear that the future of cryptocurrency security is both promising and challenging. Emerging technologies like biometric security systems and decentralized identity verification offer exhilarating possibilities for enhancing security, while ongoing education and community engagement are vital for maintaining it. As we continue to navigate this dynamic field, staying informed and proactive in our security practices will be crucial for safeguarding our digital assets against evolving threats. Looking forward, the next chapter will explore the real-world applications of Bitcoin, showcasing how this revolutionary technology is being used across various sectors to create a more connected and efficient global economy.

Chapter 8

Real-World Bitcoin Use Cases

Imagine walking into your favorite coffee shop, where the aroma of freshly brewed coffee envelops you. As you get ready to pay, instead of pulling out cash or a card, you simply scan a QR code with your smartphone and pay with Bitcoin. This isn't a glimpse into a distant future; it's a reality today in many parts of the world. Bitcoin, often revered for its investment value, is increasingly becoming a part of everyday transactions, from buying coffee to paying for services. In this chapter, we'll explore how Bitcoin is weaving itself into the fabric of daily commerce across the globe, enhancing the convenience of transactions and fostering financial inclusion in underbanked communities.

Everyday Uses of Bitcoin Around the World

Bitcoin's journey from a niche digital asset to a widely accepted medium of exchange is nothing short of remarkable. Businesses and consumers worldwide are adopting Bitcoin, drawn by its benefits such as lower transaction fees and the ease of cross-border transactions. Unlike traditional banking transactions, which may be costly and slow, especially internationally, Bitcoin transactions can be completed swiftly and without hefty fees. This is because Bitcoin transactions bypass banks and directly connect buyers and sellers.

The adoption of Bitcoin by merchants and retailers is on the rise, driven by the desire to tap into a global customer base and reduce transaction costs. From small cafes and independent artisans to large online platforms, businesses are finding Bitcoin an attractive alternative to conventional payment methods. For instance, a boutique in Tokyo might accept Bitcoin to cater to tech-savvy tourists, while an online software vendor in the U.S. might do so to avoid the fees associated with credit card transactions. These businesses will not only enjoy reduced costs but also gain access to a broader, more diverse customer base that prefers using digital currencies.

Moreover, Bitcoin is making significant inroads in underbanked regions of the world, where traditional banking services are scarce or non-existent. In many parts of Africa and Southeast Asia, people are using Bitcoin to conduct transactions and store value. Unlike banks, Bitcoin does not require a physical presence or extensive documentation to access. Anyone with a smartphone and an internet connection can set up a Bitcoin wallet and start transacting. This accessibility is revolutionizing financial participation and empowerment in these regions, offering people more control over their financial lives.

However, the adoption of Bitcoin is not without challenges. Unpredictability in its value can make day-to-day transactions tricky. If the price of Bitcoin declines after being accepted as payment, a merchant might find themselves at a loss. Similarly, consumers might hesitate to spend Bitcoin if they expect its value to increase. To address these challenges, solutions like the Lightning Network are emerging. This technology enables faster and cheaper transactions on a separate layer of the Bitcoin blockchain, making it more practical for everyday transactions. By mitigating the issues of transaction speed and costs, technologies like the Lightning Network are making Bitcoin a more practical decision for everyday use.

As it continues to evolve, Bitcoin's role in daily transactions is only expected to grow. With advancements in technology and more stable regulatory environments, we might soon see a world where Bitcoin is as common in our daily lives as traditional money. Whether it's paying for a meal, sending money across borders, or accessing financial services, Bitcoin is set to transform how we think about and use money in our everyday lives.

Bitcoin in E-commerce: A Growing Trend

The digital marketplace is buzzing, not just with consumers clicking through an overabundance of products but also through the increasing incorporation of Bitcoin as a payment method. This trend is reshaping e-commerce, providing both businesses and consumers with advantages that stretch beyond conventional monetary transactions. For businesses, Bitcoin offers a reduction in chargeback fraud. Unlike credit card payments, Bitcoin transactions, once confirmed by the network, are irreversible, effectively quashing fraudulent claims of non-delivery or unsatisfactory service after the goods have been received. For consumers, the allure lies in enhanced privacy; Bitcoin purchases do not require the disclosure of personal financial information, which reduces the risk of identity theft, something all too common in online shopping environments.

Consider the case of Overstock.com, one of the first major online retailers to welcome Bitcoin back in 2014. This move not only widened their market reach but also decreased transaction costs compared to traditional credit card payments. The system they use, a Bitcoin payment gateway, seamlessly converts Bitcoin into the store's base currency at the point of sale, protecting them from price unpredictability. This setup exemplifies a successful integration of cryptocurrency into existing financial operations, offering insight into how other platforms might adopt similar strategies.

However, integrating Bitcoin into e-commerce is not without challenges. Price volatility remains a significant hurdle. The value of Bitcoin can dramatically fluctuate within short periods, potentially complicating pricing and profitability. To lessen this problem, many businesses convert Bitcoin payments into fiat currency immediately upon receipt, thus sidestepping any potential devaluation if the market takes a downturn. Regulatory uncertainty also poses a challenge, as the legal landscape for cryptocurrencies is still evolving. Companies venturing into Bitcoin must navigate these waters carefully, staying abreast of new regulations to ensure compliance and avoid potential legal consequences.

Looking ahead, the role of Bitcoin in e-commerce appears to be ready for substantial expansion. Trends indicate a growing consumer demand for alternative payment methods that offer enhanced security and privacy. Additionally, the rise of decentralized marketplaces, platforms that operate on blockchain technology enabling peer-to-peer transactions without the need for a central authority, could further accelerate the adoption of Bitcoin in online shopping. These marketplaces not only support the use of cryptocurrencies but also align with the decentralized ethos of Bitcoin, potentially creating new e-commerce ecosystems where Bitcoin is the preferred currency.

As these trends evolve, the landscape of e-commerce will likely continue to adapt, incorporating Bitcoin not as an alternative but as a mainstay payment method that offers distinct advantages over traditional fiat currencies. The continuing developments in blockchain technology and the increasing stabilization of Bitcoin's market will play crucial roles in shaping this future, potentially transforming how we think about buying and selling in the digital age.

Bitcoin and Remittances: Facilitating Global Money Transfers

In the bustling corridors of global migration, money flows steadily from economic migrants and expatriates sending earnings back home. Traditionally, this process has been dominated by wire services and banks, often chipping away a significant chunk of hard-earned money in fees. Enter Bitcoin, a beacon of efficiency, offering a faster and cheaper channel for these cross-border money transfers. The role of Bitcoin in remittances is increasingly pivotal, especially in its ability to reduce transaction costs dramatically and speed up the process, bypassing the cumbersome and expensive intermediaries typically involved in such transfers.

One of the most profound benefits Bitcoin offers is for migrant workers and their families. Consider the scenario where a worker in the United States sends money back to their family in the Philippines. Traditional methods can be costly and slow, with fees eating into the amount sent and delays in the funds becoming available. Bitcoin changes this equation. By using Bitcoin, the worker can send money instantly at a fraction of the cost, with the family receiving it directly into their digital wallet or converting it to local currency through a local Bitcoin exchange. This immediacy can be crucial during emergencies when families back home urgently need financial support. Furthermore, these lower fees mean more of the money earned makes its way to where it's desperately needed rather than being lost to transaction fees.

The impact of this shift is palpable in specific countries where remittances form a substantial part of the economy. In El Salvador, for instance, these payments account for about 20% of the GDP. The country's move to adopt Bitcoin as legal tender is partly aimed at making it easier and cheaper for its citizens working abroad to send money home. This has not only economic but also significant social implications, enhancing the well-being of communities by boosting their disposable income, which can be spent on education, healthcare, and investment in local businesses.

However, the path of Bitcoin in remittances isn't without its hurdles, as regulatory and practical challenges abound. Different countries have variable regulations regarding the use of cryptocurrencies, affecting how easily Bitcoin can be used. For instance, while some countries like El Salvador have embraced it, others have imposed strict regulations that can complicate the use of Bitcoin. Moreover, the issue of currency conversion remains a practical challenge. While receiving money in Bitcoin is efficient, converting it to local currency can still incur costs and requires a local exchange that accepts Bitcoin. This conversion can also introduce a layer of complexity in terms of fluctuating exchange rates, which can potentially affect the final amount received.

Navigating these challenges requires a nuanced approach. In regions where regulatory hurdles are significant, advocacy for more favorable policies could be necessary. Education also plays a crucial role—both senders and receivers must understand how Bitcoin works and the best practices for using it in remittances. As for the practical challenges, the development of more robust local exchanges and the wider acceptance of Bitcoin can help mitigate these issues, making the process smoother and more beneficial for all parties involved.

As we continue to explore the evolving role of Bitcoin in the global remittance market, it's clear that its potential to transform this vital financial flow is enormous. By reducing costs and transaction times, Bitcoin not only makes it easier for workers to support their families back home but also contributes to the broader economic development of entire communities. As more countries and companies explore and adopt these processes, the area of global remittances might be poised for a significant transformation fueled by the efficiency and inclusivity offered by Bitcoin.

Philanthropy in the Bitcoin Era

In the evolving environment of giving, the emergence of Bitcoin as a tool for philanthropy is reshaping how charities and non-profit organizations interact with donors, offering a new avenue for engagement and contribution. The integration of Bitcoin into philanthropic efforts isn't just about embracing digital innovation; it's about tapping into the myriad benefits that this cryptocurrency offers, such as enhanced transparency, traceability, and accessibility. These features are particularly appealing to a sector where donors demand accountability and visibility on how their contributions are being utilized.

Charities and non-profits worldwide are increasingly accepting Bitcoin donations, drawn by the cryptocurrency's ability to provide clear, traceable records of transactions. Every Bitcoin transaction is recorded on a blockchain, offering a public, immutable ledger that tracks the flow of funds from donors to the intended projects. This level of transparency is compelling for donors who want assurance that their contributions are reaching the intended destination and being used as promised. Also, the security features inherent in blockchain technology reduce the risk of fraud, ensuring that donations are not misappropriated, a concern that can often plague charitable organizations.

The broader impact of Bitcoin on philanthropic efforts is profound. Take, for instance, the Pineapple Fund, a philanthropic initiative by an anonymous donor who pledged to donate 5,057 Bitcoins (valued at $86 million at the time) to various charitable causes. This fund supported projects across multiple sectors, including healthcare, water sanitation, and human rights. The Pineapple Fund's approach not only demonstrated the substantial impact that Bitcoin can have on philanthropy but also set a precedent for other high-net-worth individuals in the crypto community to follow suit. By providing a high-profile example of how cryptocurrencies can be leveraged for social good, the fund has encouraged more organizations to adopt this technology.

Another significant aspect of Bitcoin in philanthropy is its impact on donor engagement. Cryptocurrencies are particularly popular among younger, tech-savvy generations who are comfortable with digital technologies and value the simplicity and efficiency that digital transactions offer. For charities looking to engage this demographic, accepting Bitcoin can be an effective strategy. It aligns with the preferences of younger donors and fits seamlessly into their digital lives, making it easier for them to support causes they care about. Moreover, the novelty of using cryptocurrencies for donations can also serve as a talking point to raise awareness among potential donors, driving further engagement and support.

However, navigating the use of Bitcoin in philanthropy is not devoid of challenges. The unpredictability of Bitcoin's value can complicate fundraising efforts, as the amount received by charities can significantly fluctuate depending on the market's state at the time of the donation. To manage this, some organizations immediately convert Bitcoin donations into fiat currency to lock in the value received. Additionally, regulatory scrutiny around cryptocurrencies can pose another hurdle. The legal landscape for Bitcoin is still evolving, and organizations must ensure they remain compliant with financial regulations, which can vary significantly by jurisdiction. This includes adhering to laws related to money laundering and reporting substantial cryptocurrency transactions.

Despite these challenges, the potential of Bitcoin to transform the philanthropic sector is undeniable. As more charities and non-profits become comfortable with blockchain technology and more donors look to cryptocurrencies as a viable means of contributing to causes, we could see a significant shift in how philanthropy is conducted. This shift not only promises to make charitable giving more transparent and efficient but also more inclusive, allowing people from all over the world to participate in philanthropy regardless of their access to traditional banking systems. As we continue to explore the juncture of technology and charitable giving, Bitcoin stands out as a powerful tool that could redefine the very nature of how we support and sustain social causes around the globe.

Innovative Bitcoin Projects Making a Difference

The innovative spirit of Bitcoin doesn't stop at financial transactions. It extends into decentralized applications (DApps) that are using Bitcoin's underlying blockchain technology to revolutionize other sectors. One of the most compelling applications is in identity verification. Imagine a world where your identity is completely secure and verifiable without the risk of fraud or theft. Blockchain technology offers this possibility by creating a decentralized database of identities that is almost impossible to hack because it is stored across a network of computers, not on a single server. This application is particularly crucial in areas where identity theft is widespread and can provide a secure way to verify individual identities in multiple settings, from voting to banking.

Furthermore, the transparency and immutability of blockchain are being harnessed in supply chain management. Companies like IBM are exploring how blockchain can track the journey of goods from manufacture to sale, ensuring that every step of the process is recorded and visible. This not only helps in verifying the authenticity of the products but also enhances the efficiency of supply chains by reducing the paperwork and improving the accuracy of tracking. For instance, a luxury item like a designer bag can be traced back to its origins, reassuring the customer of its authenticity and ethical manufacture.

Turning our attention to microfinance, Bitcoin is taking significant steps to provide financial services to small businesses in developing countries. These regions often suffer from a lack of access to traditional banking services, which can stifle economic growth and entrepreneurship. Bitcoin, through various microfinance platforms, offers a solution by enabling small loans to be distributed directly to businesses and entrepreneurs without the need for a banking intermediary. This process not only cuts down the cost of loans but also speeds up their disbursement, empowering small businesses to grow and scale quickly. The impact of such initiatives is profound as they enhance and encourage economic development and provide an opportunity to those who are often left out of the traditional financial system.

Environmental sustainability is another area where Bitcoin-related technologies are making a mark. Blockchain technology is being used to create clearer and more efficient systems for trading carbon credits, which allow businesses to trade emissions permits or credits on a secure platform, encouraging the reduction of carbon footprints in a verifiable way. Additionally, some projects are using blockchain to track the usage and trading of renewable energy. This not only helps in promoting the use of renewable sources but also ensures that the energy being consumed is indeed green and provides a reliable way to manage and certify green energy usage.

Looking to the future, there is a vast potential for Bitcoin and its associated technologies to impact various sectors of society. As global connectivity increases and technological advancements continue, we can expect to see an expansion in the scope and scale of these projects. The decentralized nature of blockchain, the security it offers, and its ability to create transparent, unalterable records suggest that its applications could extend far beyond what we currently envision. Whether it's to improve democratic processes, enhance data security, or promote environmental sustainability, Bitcoin's technology promises significant societal transformation.

In wrapping up this exploration of Bitcoin's innovative applications, it's clear that the implications of this technology extend far beyond simple monetary transactions. From revolutionizing identity verification and supply chain management to empowering small businesses through microfinance and promoting environmental sustainability, Bitcoin is proving to be a versatile tool that could reshape many aspects of our world. As we continue to discover and develop these applications, the potential for Bitcoin to drive meaningful change across various sectors appears both immense and promising.

Chapter 9

The Cultural and Social Impact of Bitcoin

Imagine you're exploring a new continent. The landscape is diverse, opportunities are abundant, and each step reveals more about this intriguing territory. This is much like delving into the cultural and social dimensions of Bitcoin. It's not just about the financial implications—Bitcoin is reshaping how we think about, interact with, and understand money and our economic systems.

Bitcoin's Influence on Financial Literacy and Responsibility

Enhancing Understanding of Financial Systems

Bitcoin isn't just a digital currency; it's a tour guide through the complex world of financial systems, monetary policies, and the importance of financial sovereignty. For many, Bitcoin is their first encounter with concepts such as inflation, the role of central banks, or how monetary policies affect everyday economic life. By its nature, Bitcoin invites you to question and explore these topics. It reveals processes that are often hidden or taken for granted within traditional financial systems. For instance, understanding Bitcoin leads to insights into what money really is—a form of consensus agreement, not just printed bills or numbers in a bank account.

Moreover, Bitcoin shines a light on the concept of financial sovereignty—the principle that individuals should have control over their own money without interference from governments or banks. This concept encourages you to think critically about your rights and responsibilities as part of the financial system. It challenges the existing state of affairs and provides a practical framework for understanding how money moves, who controls it, and how it can be managed in a decentralized environment.

Promoting Financial Responsibility

The decentralized nature of Bitcoin does more than reduce reliance on traditional financial institutions; it actively empowers users to manage their own finances. This shift in control can lead to a heightened sense of financial responsibility. By using Bitcoin, you're not just a passive participant in your financial life but rather an active director. Every transaction you make with Bitcoin requires a conscious decision, reinforced by the need to manage your own private keys securely.

This hands-on management can lead to a deeper understanding of financial risks and security. For instance, being responsible for your own Bitcoin wallet teaches you about the safeguards needed to protect digital assets. It's a practical lesson in risk management and security, providing real-world skills that are transferable to other areas of personal finance. Furthermore, the transparency of Bitcoin's blockchain allows you to meticulously track every transaction. This visibility promotes a mindset of accountability and vigilance, which are crucial components of fiscal responsibility.

Educational Resources and Communities

The rise of Bitcoin has spurred the growth of numerous educational resources, online courses, and community forums. These platforms help clarify Bitcoin's technology and implications, making it more accessible to a broader audience. For example, online forums and social media groups offer spaces where beginners can learn from more experienced users, ask questions, and share insights. Educational websites provide structured courses that cover everything from blockchain technology basics to advanced trading strategies.

This proliferation of learning resources has standardized knowledge about Bitcoin, allowing more people to make knowledgeable decisions about participating in this new financial landscape. It fosters a culture of continuous learning and engagement, which is essential in the rapidly evolving world of cryptocurrency.

Impact on Consumer Behavior

Bitcoin is also influencing consumer behavior, particularly in how people approach savings and investments. The finite nature of Bitcoin, with its capped supply of 21 million coins, highlights its potential as a long-term investment rather than just a medium for daily transactions. For many, investing in Bitcoin is a deliberate strategy for wealth accumulation, encouraging a long-term perspective on financial growth.

This shift is evident in how Bitcoin holders—often referred to as 'HODLers,' a term derived from a misspelled "hold" in an online forum—approach their investments. The term has come to define a strategy of holding onto Bitcoin long-term, regardless of unpredictability. This reflects a broader shift in consumer behavior towards saving and a more strategic approach to investment, influenced by the underlying principles of Bitcoin.

Reflective Exercise: Assessing Your Financial Literacy

To fully appreciate the impact of Bitcoin on financial literacy, consider how your understanding of financial systems has evolved since you first learned about Bitcoin. Reflect on the following questions:

- How has Bitcoin changed your views on money and monetary policy?

- What lessons have you learned about financial responsibility through managing Bitcoin?

- How have community resources and educational materials helped you navigate the complexities of Bitcoin?

Engaging with these questions can deepen your appreciation of how Bitcoin is more than just a financial asset—it's a tool for education and empowerment in the economic realm.

Bitcoin as a Tool for Financial Inclusion

In many parts of the world, traditional banking infrastructures are either absent or significantly underdeveloped. This lack of access locks out millions from basic financial services that many of us take for granted—like saving money securely or transferring funds. Bitcoin, however, is changing this narrative by providing a digital alternative that bypasses traditional barriers. With only a smartphone and internet access, individuals can engage in financial activities that were previously out of reach. This revolutionary aspect of Bitcoin is not just about technological advancement; it's about real human impact, offering new financial opportunities to unbanked and underbanked populations.

The transformative power of Bitcoin lies in its ability to provide access to financial services with unprecedented inclusiveness. Traditional financial systems often exclude individuals based on their credit history, earnings, or geographical location. However, Bitcoin operates on a different set of rules that don't discriminate. There are no credit checks, no need for a fixed address, and no hidden fees. Instead, the minimal transaction fees associated with Bitcoin and the absence of a need for a physical banking infrastructure make it an ideal solution for many in remote or impoverished areas. This accessibility is crucial in regions where the nearest bank branch might be prohibitively far away or in areas where political or economic instability makes traditional banking a risky affair.

Let's take a closer look at specific case studies that showcase Bitcoin's role in financial inclusion. In Venezuela, for instance, hyperinflation has rendered the local currency nearly worthless, devastating savings and making everyday transactions challenging. Here, Bitcoin has become not just a means of investment but a necessary tool for daily survival. Many Venezuelans are turning to Bitcoin to preserve their savings from inflation, pay for essential goods and services, and even receive payments from abroad. This shift to digital currency is a direct response to the inadequacies of the conventional financial system to provide stability and reliability.

Similarly, in Zimbabwe, where trust in the local financial system is low due to years of currency instability and hyperinflation, Bitcoin offers an alternative for preserving wealth. The ability to transact globally using Bitcoin has opened up opportunities for individuals and businesses alike, allowing them to bypass the local currency for more stable digital alternatives. It's a vivid demonstration of how Bitcoin can provide financial security in environments where traditional systems have failed.

However, the road to financial inclusion via Bitcoin is not without its obstacles. One of the primary challenges is the issue of technological literacy. Engaging effectively with Bitcoin requires a basic understanding of digital technologies, which can be a significant barrier in regions with low internet access and educational resources. Moreover, the volatility of Bitcoin can be a double-edged sword; while it offers opportunities for significant gains, it also poses risks of substantial losses, especially for those who might not be fully aware of or able to manage these risks effectively.

Regulatory hurdles also pose a significant challenge. In some countries, the legal status of Bitcoin is still unclear or subject to restrictive regulations that can hinder its adoption and use as a tool for financial inclusion. Navigating this complex regulatory landscape requires continuous monitoring and adaptation, which can be a daunting task for individuals and businesses alike.

Despite these challenges, the potential of Bitcoin to act as a tool for financial inclusion remains vast. Its ability to transcend geographical and political barriers presents a unique opportunity to redefine access to financial services worldwide. By continuing to address the challenges of technological literacy, volatility, and regulatory constraints, Bitcoin can significantly enhance its role as a liberating force for the financially oppressed, paving the way for a more inclusive global economy.

The Sociopolitical Implications of Bitcoin

Bitcoin's emergence as a digital currency has not only been a technological or financial phenomenon but a potent tool with profound sociopolitical implications. Consider this: in an era where political activism often meets with resistance or outright censorship, Bitcoin has emerged as a powerful ally for those looking to support causes without interference. The ability to make donations that bypass traditional financial systems and governmental oversight can be groundbreaking. This attribute of Bitcoin has been particularly valuable to activists and organizations operating in environments where dissent is suppressed, and financial transactions are heavily monitored. By using Bitcoin, they can receive funding from international supporters without alerting governing authorities, ensuring the continuity of their work in challenging political climates.

The impact of Bitcoin extends beyond just facilitating discreet financial support; it challenges the very fabric of national monetary policy and sovereignty. Traditional financial systems are tightly integrated with national governments, giving these bodies substantial control over economic policies and financial monitoring. Bitcoin disrupts this by providing an alternative that operates outside of these established systems. This decentralization not only reduces government control over financial transactions but also diminishes their ability to enforce economic sanctions or freeze assets. For countries whose economies are impaired by hyperinflation or fiscal mismanagement, Bitcoin offers their citizens an alternative to preserve and control their wealth independently, thereby challenging the state's monopoly over the economy.

In conflict zones or regions under oppressive regimes, Bitcoin's role becomes even more critical. For example, in countries where sanctions restrict the flow of currency, Bitcoin provides a lifeline by enabling transactions and remittances that would otherwise be impossible. This capability not only aids in humanitarian efforts but also supports small businesses and families that rely on international support to survive in war-torn regions. Bitcoin's decentralized nature ensures that it remains accessible even when traditional banking infrastructures are compromised during conflicts or governmental crackdowns.

However, the growing use of Bitcoin does not come without debate or legal considerations. One of the most contentious issues is its use for illegal activities. Due to its anonymity, Bitcoin has been criticized for facilitating illegal transactions on the dark web. This aspect has led to global debates about the need for regulation and monitoring of cryptocurrencies. While the anonymity of Bitcoin can be seen as a freedom-enhancing feature, it also poses significant challenges for law enforcement and regulatory bodies trying to curb illegal financial flows. The balance between preserving the privacy and freedom that Bitcoin offers and ensuring it does not become a tool for criminal activities is a delicate one, requiring subtle and thoughtful regulatory approaches.

These discussions are not just theoretical; they have real-world implications for the adoption and regulation of Bitcoin globally. As it continues to grow in popularity, its sociopolitical impact is likely to expand. Whether it's reshaping how activists fund their campaigns or challenging the control that governments exert over financial systems, Bitcoin is proving to be a significant force in the global socio-economic landscape. Its continued evolution will likely spark further debate and possibly reshape aspects of global finance and governance in ways we can only begin to imagine. As we navigate this evolving landscape, the dual promise and challenge of Bitcoin remain at the forefront, marking it as a pivotal element in the broader discourse on economic freedom and state sovereignty.

Bitcoin and Its Role in the Fight Against Economic Inequality

Wealth Distribution and Accessibility

The concept of wealth distribution often conjures images of immense disparities, where the scale of balance is tipped heavily in favor of those already at the top. Traditional financial systems are often criticized for reinforcing these inequalities, making wealth accumulation a challenging feat for the underprivileged. Enter Bitcoin, a tool that not only challenges these traditional systems but also offers a radical blueprint for redistributing wealth. Its accessibility to anyone with internet access democratizes financial opportunities, irrespective of geographic location or socio-economic status. This universal accessibility is pivotal; it means that anyone, from a farmer in rural Africa to a teenager in Southeast Asia, holds the same fundamental ability to access and utilize Bitcoin.

This level of accessibility is unprecedented in the history of finance. Traditionally, factors such as credit history, income level, and even geographical location could significantly influence your ability to access financial services. Bitcoin eliminates these barriers by offering a flat playing field where your value and ability to grow financially are not determined by your circumstances at birth. These implications are profound. By providing equal access to an appreciating asset, Bitcoin allows wealth to accumulate in corners of the world previously overlooked by traditional finance, potentially leading to a more impartial distribution of global wealth.

Empowering Marginalized Communities

By not only providing accessibility, Bitcoin has been a beacon of empowerment for marginalized communities. These are groups that have historically been excluded from the financial conversation— people who, due to various systemic and bureaucratic impediments, have found themselves on the periphery of economic activities. In regions where banking infrastructure is scant or non-existent, Bitcoin provides a viable alternative for financial engagement. For instance, small communities in remote areas can engage in Bitcoin mining or trading as a form of income and leverage cryptocurrency to build and sustain their local economies.

Furthermore, Bitcoin has enabled these communities to bypass corrupt or inefficient local banking systems. In countries where inflation rates are high and local currencies unstable, Bitcoin offers a more stable store of value, allowing individuals to preserve their wealth in a way that simply isn't feasible with their national currencies. The empowerment comes from having control over one's financial destiny. This control is not just about having access to financial products but also about having the right tools to positively influence one's economic conditions.

Bitcoin and Microeconomies

The impact of Bitcoin extends to the creation and sustainability of microeconomies, especially in developing regions. Here, Bitcoin is not just a digital currency but a catalyst for economic activity. Small-scale enterprises and individual entrepreneurs use Bitcoin to facilitate transactions that would otherwise be hindered by fiat currency limitations. For example, a local artisan in a developing country can sell their goods online and accept Bitcoin as payment, which can then be used to purchase raw materials, pay for services, or even invest in community projects.

These microeconomic activities foster a cycle of economic growth and reinvestment within the community. As more people adopt Bitcoin, the ecosystem grows, strengthening the local economy and providing a buffer against economic shocks from the national economy. This self-sustaining model illustrates Bitcoin's potential not only as a financial asset but also as a tool for economic development, providing a foundation upon which communities can build long-term economic stability.

Long-term Potential for Reducing Inequality

Looking to the future, the potential of Bitcoin to reduce global economic inequality holds promise but also warrants a nuanced exploration. As adoption spreads and access to technology increases, Bitcoin's potential as an equalizing force could see significant fruition, and we can envisage a world where access to Bitcoin mitigates the wealth gap currently worsened by unequal access to profitable investment opportunities. The decentralized nature of Bitcoin means that as it becomes more integrated into the global economy, it can play a pivotal role in leveling the financial playing field.

However, the path to this future is fraught with challenges. Technological advancements are needed to make Bitcoin more accessible and user-friendly for those not traditionally tech-savvy. Education also plays a crucial role; understanding Bitcoin and its implications requires a level of financial literacy that isn't universally available. Addressing these challenges is crucial for Bitcoin to fulfill its potential as a tool for reducing economic inequality. As we continue to navigate these waters, the evolving role of Bitcoin in the global economy remains a compelling narrative in the quest for financial equity and empowerment.

Bitcoin's Impact on Traditional Financial Systems

Imagine walking into your local bank, where transactions, approvals, and services all hinge on a centralized authority — a norm that has been unquestioned for decades. Now, enter Bitcoin, the proverbial new kid on the block, offering a decentralized alternative that is quietly revolutionizing the banking and finance sectors. This isn't just a minor disruption; it's a seismic shift in how financial transactions can be conducted. Bitcoin operates on a peer-to-peer network supported by blockchain technology, which ensures transparency and security without the need for a central governing body. This paradigm shift challenges traditional banking by providing faster transaction processing times, reduced fees, and enhanced accessibility, making it an attractive alternative for consumers and businesses alike.

As Bitcoin continues to carve out its niche, traditional financial institutions are not standing idly by. Originally met with skepticism, many banks and financial companies are now actively exploring the possibilities within blockchain technology. Recognizing the potential for improved efficiency and security, some institutions have started adopting blockchain to modernize their core operations and enhance customer experiences. Others have gone a step further by introducing their own digital currencies or offering cryptocurrency-related services. These moves are strategic; they not only allow these institutions to stay relevant but also enable them to tap into the new and rapidly growing market of crypto-savvy consumers.

Additionally, Bitcoin is reshaping investment strategies and portfolios across the globe, as what was once viewed as a fringe asset is now being taken seriously by individual investors and large financial entities alike. With its potential for high returns, even though accompanied by high volatility, Bitcoin is increasingly seen as a legitimate asset class. Investment funds specializing in cryptocurrencies are becoming more common, and traditional investors are diversifying their portfolios to include digital currencies. This shift is not just about capitalizing on financial gains but also about hedging against potential risks associated with traditional financial systems, such as inflation or geopolitical instabilities.

Exploring potential future scenarios for the coexistence of Bitcoin and traditional financial systems reveals a range of possibilities influenced by regulatory developments, technological advancements, and market integration. One scenario could see Bitcoin becoming a mainstream financial asset, integrating seamlessly into existing financial infrastructures. Banks might act as safe-keepers of digital assets, and Bitcoin could be used for daily transactions as well as long-term investments. Alternatively, if regulatory challenges become too great or if the volatility of Bitcoin remains high, it might remain a niche asset favored by a smaller group of enthusiasts and investors.

As we reflect on these developments, it's clear that Bitcoin is not just a passing trend but a significant player in the evolution of financial systems. Its continued impact on traditional banking, reactions from financial institutions, and shifts in investment strategies underscore a broader movement towards a more decentralized and digital financial landscape. This evolution isn't just about technology; it's about reimagining and reshaping the financial norms that have been in place for centuries.

As we close this chapter on Bitcoin's impact on traditional financial systems, we uncover how deep the roots of this digital currency are growing into the very foundation of financial practices. From disrupting the way banks operate to altering investment paradigms, Bitcoin is undeniably carving its path forward. As we step into the next chapter, we'll explore the technological underpinnings that make Bitcoin a unique and powerful player in the financial world, setting the stage for a deeper understanding of its mechanisms and potential.

Chapter 10

Looking Ahead: The Future of Bitcoin

Imagine the world of finance as a vast ocean, where traditional banking systems have long sailed as the predominant ships, guiding economic trade and monetary control. Now, picture Bitcoin and other cryptocurrencies as innovative, swift boats, zipping around and between these giant ships, empowered by the winds of technology and change. This chapter is about charting the course of these nimble crafts, exploring how they're not only navigating the waters but actively changing the tide of how financial transactions are conducted globally.

Emerging Trends in Bitcoin and Cryptocurrency

Integration with Financial Technologies

The integration of Bitcoin with developing financial technologies, particularly neobanks and fintech platforms, is akin to adding turbo engines to traditional banking vehicles. Neobanks, operating solely online without physical branches, embodies the synergy between digital banking and cryptocurrencies. They offer streamlined, user-friendly interfaces and cost-effective services, making them attractive to tech-savvy consumers who value convenience and efficiency. By integrating Bitcoin, these platforms not only expand their service offerings but also embrace the ethos of decentralized financial control and reduced reliance on traditional financial infrastructures. This fusion represents a significant shift in how you, as a consumer, can manage your finances—transcending international borders and accessing a global economic network at your fingertips.

Moreover, fintech platforms that incorporate Bitcoin are pushing the envelope in terms of offering innovative services like instant cross-border payments, micro-loans, and peer-to-peer transactions with reduced fees. These platforms are not only adopting Bitcoin for its novelty; they are harnessing its underlying blockchain technology to enhance security, increase transparency, and improve the efficiency of their operations. This trend is setting a new standard in the financial sector, prompting traditional banks to rethink their strategies and potentially adopt similar technologies to stay competitive.

Advancements in Scalability Solutions

Scalability is one of the most significant challenges Bitcoin faces, particularly the speed and cost of transactions. As Bitcoin continues to grow in popularity, the need for it to handle a larger volume of transactions is imperative. Currently, solutions like the Lightning Network, which operates as a second layer over the Bitcoin blockchain, are instrumental in addressing these issues. The Lightning Network allows for quicker and more cost-efficient transactions by enabling off-chain transactions, which are settled on the blockchain once the user decides to close out the channel. This method significantly reduces the burden on the main blockchain, allowing for increased transaction throughput.

Looking ahead, further advancements are expected in scalability solutions. Globally, developers and engineers are working on various upgrades and third-party solutions that promise to enhance

Bitcoin's ability to handle a growing volume of transactions while maintaining security and decentralization. These advancements are crucial for Bitcoin's adoption as a mainstream form of currency and can potentially revolutionize other areas of finance, such as real-time, large-scale transaction processing and microtransactions in internet-of-things applications.

The Role of Artificial Intelligence

Artificial Intelligence (AI) is set to play a transformative role in the evolution of Bitcoin and cryptocurrency. AI algorithms can analyze vast amounts of data from Bitcoin transactions to detect patterns, predict market trends, and identify potential security threats. This capability is incredibly beneficial for both individual investors and institutional players, as it can lead to more informed decision-making and enhanced risk management.

Besides, AI can automate complex processes such as compliance checks, wallet management, and customer support, making cryptocurrency platforms more user-friendly and efficient. As AI technology advances, its integration with Bitcoin could lead to more adaptive, intelligent, and responsive financial services, where transactions are not only secure and fast but also vigorously optimized for market conditions.

Influence of Institutional Adoption

The increasing interest in and adoption of Bitcoin by institutional investors and large corporations marks a significant milestone in its journey toward mainstream acceptance. This trend is indicative of Bitcoin's maturing market and perceived potential as a stable investment asset. Institutional involvement brings considerable market liquidity and stability, which can lead to more regulated and structured cryptocurrency markets.

As institutions integrate Bitcoin into their financial strategies, we can expect an increase in innovative financial products related to cryptocurrencies, such as Bitcoin futures, options, and ETFs, providing both retail and institutional investors with various investment opportunities. The influence of institutional adoption extends beyond investment portfolios; it validates Bitcoin's legitimacy as a financial asset and paves the way for broader market acceptance and integration into the global economic system.

As we steer through these emerging trends, the interplay between Bitcoin and advancing technologies paints a promising horizon, along with its integration into the broader financial ecosystem. The journey of Bitcoin is far from over; it's evolving, growing, and continuously reshaping the landscape of finance. As you navigate your own financial journey, staying informed and adaptable to these changes can not only enhance your understanding of Bitcoin but also empower you to make more strategic investment decisions in this dynamic digital age.

The Sustainability of Bitcoin Mining

When it comes to Bitcoin mining, the imagery that often springs to mind might be rows of machines whirring away, consuming vast amounts of electrical power. This scene has raised significant environmental concerns, given the substantial energy required to maintain the Bitcoin network. However, it's not just about energy consumption; it's also about the innovations and community actions aimed at steering Bitcoin mining towards a more sustainable future.

Let's delve into how the evolving landscape of Bitcoin mining is addressing its environmental impact and the role that regulatory and technological advancements are playing in this change.

The environmental impact of Bitcoin mining has been a hot topic, sparking debates and urging miners and the broader community to consider greener practices. One of the most promising developments in this area is the increasing adoption of renewable energy sources in mining operations. Solar, wind, and hydroelectric power are becoming more widespread as energy sources for mining farms, particularly in regions where these resources are abundant and cheap. This shift not only helps reduce the carbon footprint associated with Bitcoin mining but also improves the overall sustainability of the mining operations. Additionally, initiatives like carbon offset programs are gaining traction. These programs allow mining companies to invest in environmental projects to compensate for their carbon emissions, creating a balance that could lead to a reduction in the overall environmental impact of the cryptocurrency mining industry.

Let's consider the regulatory landscape, which significantly influences mining practices globally. As countries become more conscious of the environmental impacts of digital currencies, regulatory bodies are stepping in to set guidelines that encourage or mandate the use of renewable energy. For instance, some regions are exploring the implementation of policies that require cryptocurrency miners to use a certain percentage of renewable energy in their operations. These regulations not only promote a shift towards sustainability but also push the industry to innovate and find new solutions in order to meet these requirements. Furthermore, the scrutiny from regulators often leads to better reporting and transparency in energy usage, which can drive a broader shift across the industry towards more sustainable practices.

Technological advancements in mining hardware are also pivotal in enhancing energy efficiency. The development of more power-efficient ASIC miners is on the rise, with manufacturers competing to create hardware that offers more hashing power with less electrical consumption. The evolution of these devices means that the same amount of cryptographic puzzles can be solved using significantly less power, reducing the overall energy requirements of the mining process. This is crucial, as improved efficiency can drastically decrease the environmental impact per transaction, making Bitcoin mining more sustainable as the network scales.

Finally, the role of community-driven initiatives cannot be understated. Across the Bitcoin network, communities are developing numerous projects and protocols to promote sustainable mining practices. These include decentralized applications that allow for transparent tracking of energy consumption and the sourcing of green energy. Furthermore, mining pools focused on renewable energy are forming, providing a platform for miners who want to reduce their environmental impact by collaborating and sharing resources. These community efforts are instrumental in pushing the envelope regarding the possibilities of making Bitcoin mining an environmentally responsible activity.

As we explore these developments, it becomes clear that the narrative around Bitcoin mining is complex and evolving. The industry is at a crossroad where environmental sustainability is becoming just as important as profitability. With the collective efforts of miners, regulators, technologists, and the global community, the future of

Bitcoin mining looks not only greener but also more sustainable and efficient. This shift is crucial, not just in regard to reducing the environmental impact but also to ensure the long-term viability of Bitcoin as a leading digital currency.

Predicting the Long-term Value of Bitcoin

Predicting the future value of Bitcoin is a bit like forecasting the weather in an unfamiliar climate. There are observable patterns and a wealth of data, but the occasional storm can come out of nowhere, drastically altering the landscape. Over the long term, several factors are likely to influence Bitcoin's value: technological advancements, regulatory changes, market adoption, and macroeconomic factors. These elements intertwine in complex ways, making the cryptocurrency's future both fascinating and unpredictable.

Technological advancements play a pivotal role, particularly as Bitcoin continues to evolve. Innovations that enhance the scalability, security, and usability of Bitcoin will likely push its value upward. For instance, improvements in blockchain technology that allow for faster processing and verification of transactions can make Bitcoin more attractive to both consumers and businesses, increasing its utility as a medium of exchange. While advancements in cryptographic security might make Bitcoin even more secure, it's an essential factor when considering the increasing sophistication of cyber threats. As these technologies mature, they enhance the intrinsic value of Bitcoin, making it a more reliable and robust asset.

Regulatory changes are also significant influencers. As governments around the world better understand cryptocurrency, their approach to regulation will likely evolve. Positive regulatory frameworks can increase investor confidence and broaden Bitcoin's appeal to a broader audience, including institutional investors. On the other hand, stringent regulations may impose operational challenges, potentially stifling growth and innovation within the cryptocurrency space. However, it's also possible that hardship from tight regulations could foster innovative solutions that might circumvent or mitigate these challenges, thereby strengthening the ecosystem.

Market adoption encompasses everything from the acceptance of Bitcoin by merchants and consumers for daily transactions to its use by corporations and governments as a reserve asset. Widespread adoption hinges on Bitcoin's volatility, transaction fees, and ease of use, all of which are areas expected to improve with technological advancements and regulatory clarity. If Bitcoin were to become a standard for daily transactions or a reserve currency, this would significantly enhance its value, providing a stable demand base that could lead to price stabilization and increased valuation.

However, we cannot overlook the influence of macroeconomic factors, such as inflation rates, currency devaluation, and economic recessions. In environments where traditional fiat currencies are unstable, Bitcoin may be seen as a safer asset to store value, similar to gold. This perspective was particularly evident during high inflation periods in countries like Venezuela and Zimbabwe, where Bitcoin adoption saw substantial increases. If global economies face recession or significant financial crises, Bitcoin could similarly gain traction as a hedge against economic uncertainty.

Incorporating insights from financial analysts, economists, and blockchain experts provides a broader perspective on Bitcoin's potential financial trajectories. Many experts believe that as long as the fundamental aspects of Bitcoin, such as its decentralized nature, fixed supply, and increasing demand, continue to be relevant, it will maintain a significant value. Others caution about the speculative nature of cryptocurrencies and suggest a more conservative approach. These expert analyses are crucial as they provide grounded perspectives that balance the often polarized views found in general discourse.

As we consider the various scenarios of Bitcoin adoption—ranging from its use in daily transactions to becoming a reserve currency—the potential impacts on its value are profound. In a world where Bitcoin achieves widespread transactional use, we might see it becoming more stable, akin to traditional fiat currencies, but with an advantage due to its lower transaction costs and borderless nature. On the other hand, if Bitcoin were to be adopted as a reserve currency by even a small number of countries, the increase in demand and the consequential reduction in supply could drive its value significantly higher.

Each scenario presents a fascinating glimpse into the potential future of Bitcoin, colored by technological, regulatory, and economic factors. As you navigate the landscape of cryptocurrency investment, keeping an eye on these indicators can provide valuable insights into how Bitcoin might evolve and what that could mean for its value. Whether you're considering investing in Bitcoin or are simply curious about its prospects, understanding these dynamics is essential for anyone looking to grasp the potential of this groundbreaking digital asset.

How Bitcoin Could Shape the Future of Global Economies

Imagine a bustling digital marketplace where Bitcoin is not just a currency but a foundational element that influences how transactions are conducted, identities are verified, and businesses operate across borders. In this evolving digital economy, Bitcoin's role extends beyond a mere tool for financial transactions; it becomes a catalyst for redefining interactions in the online world. The integration of Bitcoin into digital identities is a significant advancement, providing a more protected and immutable method of handling identity verification processes. This could drastically reduce the instances of identity theft and fraud, making online spaces safer for users and businesses alike.

Likewise, Bitcoin's influence on online marketplaces could revolutionize e-commerce. By facilitating direct, peer-to-peer transactions without the need for intermediaries, Bitcoin could lower transaction fees, increase transaction speed, and open up global markets to sellers and buyers who previously had limited access due to financial barriers or restrictive banking regulations. This level of economic democratization could significantly alter the landscape of global trade, making it more inclusive and accessible to many. Additionally, Bitcoin's ability to effortlessly execute cross-border transactions at lower costs could transform international trade, allowing businesses and entrepreneurs in less developed economies to participate more fully in the global market.

The challenges Bitcoin poses to the traditional financial system are profound. By offering an alternate to government-issued currencies, Bitcoin questions the monopoly of national central banks on money supply and control. This could lead to shifts in global financial power dynamics, particularly if countries with unstable currencies see their citizens switch to Bitcoin or other cryptocurrencies. Such a shift could weaken the control those governments have over their national economies and spur changes in how global financial policies are crafted.

Bitcoin's potential to globally democratize economic participation is one of its most compelling aspects. By providing equal access to financial tools and resources, Bitcoin can level the playing field for people in different regions and socioeconomic backgrounds. Where access to traditional banking is limited or non-existent, Bitcoin can offer a viable alternative for storing value, making transactions, and even accessing credit. This could lead to increased economic activity and entrepreneurship, particularly in developing countries where a significant portion of the population is without access to banks.

The long-term socioeconomic impacts of Bitcoin could be transformative if its adoption continues to grow. Changes in the distribution of wealth are likely as Bitcoin and other cryptocurrencies provide new opportunities for wealth accumulation outside of traditional financial systems, which have often been criticized for favoring the already wealthy. Economic policies might need to be reevaluated and adapted to accommodate the rise of digital currencies, which do not respect national boundaries and are not easily controlled by any single entity. International trade practices may also evolve as cryptocurrencies like Bitcoin make it easier and cheaper to conduct transactions across borders. This could lead to a more interconnected and interdependent global economy where the traditional barriers of currency exchange and trade regulations are less significant.

As we look to the future, the potential of Bitcoin to reshape global economies is both exciting and challenging. Its role in the digital economy, its challenge to traditional financial systems, its potential for democratizing economic participation, and its long-term socioeconomic impacts are all areas that warrant close attention. Understanding these dynamics is crucial for anyone interested in the future of finance, technology, and global economic policy.

As this chapter closes, we reflect on the transformative potential of Bitcoin and its possible impacts on our global economic systems. The discussions here lead us to the broader consideration of digital currency's role in future societal structures, which will be explored further in the coming chapters. With each step forward, we inch closer to understanding the profound changes that Bitcoin could bring to our world.

Conclusion

As we wrap up our journey through the fascinating world of Bitcoin, from its humble beginnings amidst the 2008 financial crisis to its current stature as a pivotal force in global finance, it's clear that Bitcoin is more than just a digital currency. It has emerged as a formidable challenge to traditional financial systems. It is a tool for enhancing financial inclusion, as well as a catalyst for expanding financial literacy across the globe.

Bitcoin was created not just as an alternative investment asset but as a means to empower individuals with the independence to manage their financial resources without reliance on centralized institutions. Its potential to democratize access to financial services worldwide is one of its most compelling attributes, offering a beacon of hope for millions who are currently underserved by conventional banking systems.

Throughout this book, we've explored how Bitcoin is transforming financial literacy, with its underlying technologies making it more accessible and secure for users around the world. We've delved into the significant role Bitcoin plays in the economy and touched upon the environmental impacts of Bitcoin mining, acknowledging the community's ongoing efforts to address these challenges.

Here are the key takeaways: Bitcoin is not just a form of money or an investment but a movement towards a more equitable financial system. The importance of maintaining robust security in your Bitcoin investments cannot be overstated, and the need for continual education in this rapidly evolving sector is crucial.

I urge you to not just be a bystander but to actively engage in the Bitcoin ecosystem. Start small by investing a manageable amount, participate in online communities, and advocate for Bitcoin's adoption within your networks. Your involvement not only enriches your understanding but also contributes to the broader acceptance and success of Bitcoin.

The dynamic nature of Bitcoin and cryptocurrency means that staying informed is crucial. Keep abreast of developments by following reputable news sources, participating in forums, and utilizing a variety of educational materials. This ongoing learning process will help you navigate the complexities of the cryptocurrency world more effectively.

Reflect on how Bitcoin can influence broader socioeconomic issues and consider how you can be part of this transformative wave. Every individual action, whether it's using Bitcoin for transactions, investing, or simply educating others, plays a role in shaping our financial future.

Thank you sincerely for joining me on this enlightening exploration of Bitcoin. Your engagement and willingness to learn about this groundbreaking technology are what drive its ongoing evolution and success. I invite you to share your thoughts, experiences, and insights as you venture further into the world of Bitcoin investing and utilization.

Looking ahead, the future of Bitcoin is ripe with possibilities. While uncertainties remain, the potential for Bitcoin to forge a more inclusive, efficient, and transparent financial landscape is a vision that holds remarkable promise. Let's continue to watch, participate, and influence this exciting financial revolution.

Here's to taking control of our financial destinies and being part of a future where finance is genuinely global, decentralized, and accessible to all.

References

- *The 2008 global meltdown and the birth of Bitcoin - Mint* https://www.livemint.com/Money/YTYMYUD7dytGK5PGSpdRTN/The-2008-global-meltdown-and-the-birth-of-Bitcoin.html

- *Blockchain: What It Is, How It Works, Why It Matters* https://builtin.com/blockchain

- *What Is Bitcoin Mining?* https://www.investopedia.com/terms/b/bitcoin-mining.asp

- *Cryptocurrency vs. Traditional Banking: Understanding the Differences and Benefits* https://www.globaltrademag.com/cryptocurrency-vs-traditional-banking-understanding-the-differences-and-benefits/

- *The History of Money: Bartering to Banknotes to Bitcoin* https://www.investopedia.com/articles/07/roots_of_money.asp

- *Decentralized Finance Will Change Your Understanding Of ...* https://www.forbes.com/sites/philippsandner/2021/02/22/decentralized-finance-will-change-your-understanding-of-financial-systems/

- *Venezuela's Bitcoin Story Puts It in a Category of One* https://www.coindesk.com/business/2020/11/11/venezuelas-bitcoin-story-puts-it-in-a-category-of-one/

- *How Banks Are Adapting to Cryptocurrency* https://alphapoint.com/blog/banks-and-cryptocurrency/

- *How to choose the best Bitcoin wallet | Get Started with ...* https://www.bitcoin.com/get-started/how-to-choose-the-right-bitcoin-wallet/

- *How To Buy Bitcoin - Investopedia* https://www.investopedia.com/articles/investing/082914/basics-buying-and-investing-bitcoin.asp

- *What To Know About Cryptocurrency and Scams* https://consumer.ftc.gov/articles/what-know-about-cryptocurrency-and-scams

- *Bitcoin and the Predictability of Crypto Market Cycles* https://www.coindesk.com/markets/2023/12/06/bitcoin-and-the-predictability-of-crypto-market-cycles/

- *The Impact of Global Events on Cryptocurrency Valuations* https://zenledger.io/blog/the-impact-of-global-events-on-cryptocurrency-valuations/

- *12 Bitcoin Success Stories: Meet Bitcoin Millionaires* https://www.cointree.com/learn/bitcoin-success-stories/

- *Crypto Technical Analysis: Techniques, Indicators, and ...* https://onetrading.com/blogs/crypto-technical-analysis-techniques-indicators-and-applications

- *What Is Bitcoin Mining?* https://www.investopedia.com/terms/b/bitcoin-mining.asp

- *What Is the Bitcoin Hashrate and Why Does It Matter?* https://unchainedcrypto.com/what-is-the-bitcoin-hashrate/

- *Lightning Network: What It Is and How It Works* https://www.investopedia.com/terms/l/lightning-network.asp

- *What is the Future of Blockchain and Cryptocurrencies* https://online.stanford.edu/future-blockchain-and-cryptocurrencies

- *Countries Where Bitcoin Is Legal and Illegal* https://www.investopedia.com/articles/forex/041515/countries-where-bitcoin-legal-illegal.asp

- *How Does The SEC Regulate Crypto?* https://www.forbes.com/advisor/investing/cryptocurrency/sec-crypto-regulation/

- *Crypto Wrestles With Legal Issues, Scoring A Few Key Victories in 2023* https://www.forbes.com/sites/digital-assets/2023/12/27/crypto-wrestles-with-legal-issues-scoring-a-few-key-victories-in-2023/

- *Bitcoin Security: Here's What Makes The OG Blockchain Safer Than Fort Knox* https://finimize.com/content/bitcoin-security-heres-what-makes-the-og-blockchain-safer-than-fort-knox-with-ledger

- *What To Know About Cryptocurrency and Scams* https://consumer.ftc.gov/articles/what-know-about-cryptocurrency-and-scams

- *Cryptocurrency Security: Best Practices for Protecting Your ...* https://cardsrealm.com/en-us/articles/cryptocurrency-security-best-practices-for-protecting-your-investments

- *What is the Future of Blockchain and Cryptocurrencies* https://online.stanford.edu/future-blockchain-and-cryptocurrencies

- *Bitcoin Adoption: Number of Merchants Accepting BTC Payments 2023* https://www.coinspeaker.com/bitcoin-adoption-btc-payments-2023/

- *Case Study: Should We Embrace Crypto?* https://hbr.org/2021/11/case-study-should-we-embrace-crypto

- *Why Bitcoin Mining Might Actually Be Great For Sustainability* https://www.forbes.com/sites/digital-assets/2023/09/21/why-bitcoin-mining-might-actually-be-great-for-sustainability/

- *Cryptocurrency Adoption in Developing Countries* https://www.bitstamp.net/learn/crypto-101/cryptocurrency-adoption-in-developing-countries/

- *The Impact of Cryptocurrency on Traditional Banking* https://www.financemagnates.com/thought-leadership/the-impact-of-cryptocurrency-on-traditional-banking/

- *Open-source Bitcoin education aims to spread global financial literacy* https://cointelegraph.com/news/open-source-bitcoin-education-global-financial-literacy

- *Cryptocurrency Regulations Around the World* https://www.investopedia.com/cryptocurrency-regulations-around-the-world-5202122

- *The Future of Bitcoin Beyond 2024: Challenges and ...* https://aibc.world/learn-crypto-hub/future-of-bitcoin/

- *Bitcoin Scalability: Challenges and Solutions* https://crypto.com/university/bitcoin-scalability

- *UN Study Reveals the Hidden Environmental Impacts of ...* https://unu.edu/press-release/un-study-reveals-hidden-environmental-impacts-bitcoin-carbon-not-only-harmful-product

- *Bitcoin Price Prediction In 2024: Boom Or Bust?* https://www.forbes.com/advisor/investing/cryptocurrency/bitcoin-price-prediction-2024/